By M.T.T

I0427420

Six Numbers to Freedom: Your Roadmap to Winning the American Lotter

CRACKiNG THE CODE TO FiNANCiAL LiBERATiON

Disclaimer:

While every effort has been made by the author to ensure the accuracy and completeness of the information contained in this book, the author assumes no responsibility for any errors or omissions. This book is not intended to be a substitute for professional legal or investigative advice. Readers are advised to consult a qualified professional for assistance with specific legal or investigative matters.

Table of content

Part 1: The Lottery Landscape: Charting Your Course to Fortune

Have you ever dreamt of numbers dancing on a screen, transforming your life in an instant? The American lottery, with its promise of life-altering jackpots, beckons millions with its tantalizing allure. But before you dive headfirst into the world of quick picks and lucky charms, there's crucial terrain to navigate: the lottery landscape.

This introductory section serves as your compass, guiding you through the intricate pathways of the American lottery system. We'll delve into the diverse tapestry of games available, from multi-state behemoths to state-specific gems, each with its unique rules, odds, and payouts. Understanding these differences is paramount, as they can significantly impact your chances of winning and the size of your potential windfall.

But the journey doesn't end there. We'll also explore the often-overlooked yet crucial aspect of responsible lottery play. Setting realistic expectations, managing your budget wisely, and understanding the potential impact of a win – these are cornerstones of a successful lottery journey. By laying a solid foundation, you'll ensure that your lottery experience is not just about chasing dreams, but about doing so with informed awareness and responsible choices.

So, are you ready to embark on this exciting exploration? Buckle up, because Part 1: The Lottery Landscape is about to equip you with the knowledge and understanding to navigate this world with confidence and potentially, change your life forever.

Chapter 1: Demystifying the Maze: Understanding the American Lottery System

The American lottery system shimmers with the promise of instant wealth, but beneath the glitz lies a complex landscape with diverse games, varying rules, and ever-shifting odds. Before you pick your first numbers, diving into this intricate world is essential. In this chapter, we'll serve as your guide, unraveling the mysteries and equipping you with the knowledge to make informed decisions.

First, we'll embark on a tour of the different lottery games available, from the behemoths like Powerball and Mega Millions to state-specific offerings with unique twists. We'll break down their rules, from number selection formats to drawing schedules, ensuring you understand the mechanics of each game.

Next, we'll delve into the heart of the matter: odds. Prepare to grapple with probability; we'll explore the mathematical realities of winning, dissecting how factors like the number of balls drawn and prize structures affect your chances. Don't worry, we'll make it clear and understandable, even for those who haven't met statistics with open arms.

But knowledge doesn't stop at numbers and games. We'll also unveil the often-overlooked aspect of taxes. Understanding how much Uncle Sam takes from your windfall is crucial for realistic planning and budgeting.

By the end of this chapter, you'll have a clear picture of the American lottery system, its intricacies and realities. You'll be able to choose the game that aligns with your risk tolerance and understand the odds you're facing. Remember, knowledge is power, and in the lottery world, it can be the difference between chasing a dream and making an informed choice.

So, are you ready to step into the lottery landscape with newfound clarity? Let's begin!

Different Lottery Games and Their Rules: Navigating the Options

The American lottery landscape is a tapestry woven with diverse games, each offering its own unique set of rules and potential rewards. In this section, we'll unravel the threads, providing a comprehensive overview of the most popular options:

Multi-State Games:
Powerball:
The undisputed kingpin, boasting massive jackpots and requiring players to match five white balls from 1 to 69 and one red Powerball from 1 to 26.
- **Mega Millions:**

Another heavyweight, featuring a similar format with five white balls from 1 to 70 and one gold Mega Ball from 1 to 25.
- **Lucky for Life:**

Offering a lifetime annuity instead of a lump sum, players match five white balls from 1 to 47 and one green Lucky Ball from 1 to 18.

State-Specific Games :
- **Pick-3, Pick-4, Pick-5:**

These offer smaller jackpots but higher winning odds, requiring players to match 3, 4, or 5 numbers drawn from a smaller pool. Rules and payouts vary by state.
- **Cash 4 Life, Mega Millions Multiplier:**

Variations on popular games with additional features like multipliers or second-chance drawings, often with different rules and odds.
- **Scratch-Offs:**

Instant win tickets with various themes and prizes, offering immediate gratification but lower overall odds compared to drawn games.

Navigating the Rules:
- **Draw Schedules:**

Each game has its own draw schedule, usually twice a week for multi-state games and more frequent for state-specific options.
- **Ticket Prices:**

Prices vary depending on the game and options like additional features.
- **Matching Requirements:**

Understanding how many numbers need to match and in what order is crucial.

- **Jackpot Rollovers:**

When jackpots go unclaimed, they increase, influencing the potential payout and overall odds.

Remember: This is just a glimpse into the diverse world of lottery games. Always research the specific rules and details of the game you choose before playing.

Unveiling the Odds: A Reality Check on Winning and Jackpots

The allure of the lottery lies in the possibility of instant wealth, but before diving in, it's crucial to confront the reality: the odds of winning are incredibly low. In this section, we'll delve into the mathematical realities, examining the odds of winning different prizes and the varying jackpot sizes across different games.

Odds of Winning:
- **Understanding Probability:**

We'll break down the mathematical concepts behind odds, explaining how factors like the number of balls and possible combinations influence your chances.

- **Jackpot Odds:**

Prepare for a stark reality check. We'll reveal the true odds of winning the jackpot, often exceeding hundreds of millions to one, making it a true long shot.

- **Smaller Prizes:**

While the jackpot may be elusive, there are often multiple prize tiers with better odds. We'll explore the odds of winning these smaller prizes, helping you manage expectations.

Jackpot Sizes:
- **Variation Across Games:**

Jackpot sizes vary significantly across different games. We'll compare and contrast the starting and potential maximum jackpots for popular games like Powerball and Mega Millions.

- **Rollover Impact:**

When jackpots go unclaimed, they increase, attracting more players and inflating the potential payout. We'll explain how rollovers affect both the jackpot size and your odds of winning.

- **Taxes and Take-Home Pay:**

Don't forget Uncle Sam! We'll explore the tax implications of lottery winnings, ensuring you understand how much you'll actually take home after taxes.

Remember: The key takeaway from this section is to approach the lottery with realistic expectations. While winning the jackpot is a dream, understanding the true odds and potential payouts will help you make informed decisions and avoid chasing unrealistic fantasies.

Next Up: We'll explore the crucial aspect of responsible lottery play, helping you set limits, manage your budget, and enjoy the game without compromising your financial well-being.

Facing the Taxman: Understanding Lottery Winnings and Taxes

Imagine winning the lottery, only to discover a significant chunk disappears before it even reaches your hands. That's the harsh reality of taxes on lottery winnings. This section will equip you with the knowledge to navigate this complex terrain and maximize your post-tax windfall.

Federal Tax Bite:
- **Ordinary Income:**

Uncle Sam considers lottery winnings ordinary income, subject to the same tax rates as your salary. We'll explain the current federal tax brackets and how they translate to your potential tax burden.

- **Withholding at Source:**

Most lottery agencies withhold 24% of winnings exceeding $5,000 for federal taxes. However, this might not cover your full tax obligation, leaving you with a potential tax bill later.

State and Local Taxes:
- **State Variations:**

Different states have varying tax rates on lottery winnings, ranging from 0% to over 10%. We'll provide resources to research your state's specific tax rate.

- **Local Taxes:**

In some cases, local jurisdictions may also impose additional taxes on lottery winnings.

Planning for Tax Implications:

- **Seek Professional Advice:**

Consulting a tax professional before claiming your prize is highly recommended. They can guide you through the intricacies of tax laws and ensure you minimize your tax burden.

- **Estimated Tax Payments:**

Depending on your overall income and the size of your winnings, you may need to make estimated tax payments throughout the year. We'll explain how to avoid penalties and ensure you stay compliant.

- **Tax-Saving Strategies:**

While limited, there might be potential tax-saving strategies available. We'll discuss these options with the caveat that responsible financial planning should always be the priority.

Remember: Taxes are an unavoidable reality of lottery winnings. By understanding the tax implications and planning accordingly, you can ensure you maximize your take-home pay and avoid any unexpected surprises come tax season.

Moving Forward:

With this knowledge in your arsenal, you're now equipped to navigate the complex world of lottery taxes. Next, we'll delve into the crucial topic of choosing the right game for you, considering your budget, risk tolerance, and desired outcome.

Chapter 2: Choosing Your Champion: Navigating the Lottery Game Arena

Now that you've demystified the American lottery landscape, it's time to pick your weapon of choice: the game that aligns with your dreams, budget, and risk tolerance. In this chapter, we'll guide you through the selection process, helping you find the perfect match for your lottery aspirations.

The Game Spectrum:
- **Multi-State Giants:**

Powerball and Mega Millions offer massive jackpots but lower winning odds. Consider them if you're chasing the ultimate dream, but remember the long shot reality.

- **State-Specific Gems:**

These games have smaller jackpots but higher winning odds. Explore options like Pick-3, Pick-4, and Cash 4 Life, considering your state's specific offerings.

- **Scratch-Offs:**

Instant gratification and smaller prizes define this category. They're fun for casual play, but remember the lower overall odds compared to drawn games.

Matching Your Playstyle:
- **Dream Chaser:**

Opt for multi-state games if you dream of life-altering wealth, but manage expectations and prioritize responsible play.

- **Balanced Approach:**

Consider state-specific games with higher winning odds for smaller jackpots, offering a more realistic chance of winning while still enjoying the thrill.

- **Casual Player:**

Scratch-offs might be your choice for occasional fun, but limit your spending due to the lower overall odds.

Beyond the Jackpot:
- **Prize Tiers:**

Explore the different prize tiers offered by each game. While the jackpot may be elusive, winning smaller prizes can still be exciting and rewarding.
- **Bonus Features:**

Some games offer additional features like multipliers or second-chance drawings. Consider if these features align with your preferences and budget.
- **Draw Schedule and Frequency:**

Choose a game that fits your playing style. Do you prefer frequent draws for more chances to win, or are you okay with waiting for larger jackpots?

Remember: Choosing the right game is crucial. Don't get swept away by the allure of the biggest jackpot; prioritize responsible play and choose a game that aligns with your budget, risk tolerance, and playing style.

Next Up: We'll delve into the crucial aspect of responsible lottery play, equipping you with strategies to manage your finances and avoid the pitfalls of chasing unrealistic dreams.

Matching Games vs. Drawing Games: Picking Your Playstyle

The diverse world of lottery games offers two distinct categories: **matching games** and **drawing games**. Understanding their differences is crucial for choosing the game that aligns with your playing style and preferences. Let's delve into the key distinctions:

Matching Games:
- **Gameplay:** You're presented with a set of pre-selected numbers and need to match them exactly on your ticket.
- **Examples:** Keno, Cash 4 Life, some state-specific Pick-n games.
- **Pros:**
- **Higher winning odds**: Generally, you have a higher chance of winning smaller prizes compared to drawing games.
- **Multiple chances**: Some games offer multiple draws per day, increasing your chances to win.

- **Cons:**
- **Lower jackpots**: The maximum prizes are usually much smaller compared to drawing games.
- **Limited control**: You don't choose the numbers; your chances depend solely on luck.

Drawing Games:
- **Gameplay:** You select your own numbers from a pool, hoping they match the ones drawn during the lottery draw.
- **Examples:** Powerball, Mega Millions, most Pick-n games.
- **Pros:**
- **Massive jackpots**: The potential for life-altering wealth is the biggest draw.
- **Choose your numbers**: You have control over your selection, offering a sense of agency.
- **Cons:**
- **Extremely low winning odds**: Your chances of winning the jackpot are astronomically low.
- **Limited prize tiers**: Fewer prize tiers compared to some matching games.

Choosing Your Playstyle:
- **Dream Chaser:**
If you have your sights set on the ultimate prize, drawing games might be tempting. However, remember the low odds and prioritize responsible play.
- **Balanced Approach:**
Matching games offer a more realistic chance of winning smaller prizes while enjoying the thrill. Consider your budget and risk tolerance.
- **Casual Player:**
Both categories offer options. Match games with frequent draws and smaller prizes might suit your occasional playstyle, while scratch-offs (a type of matching game) offer instant gratification.

Remember: The choice ultimately depends on your preferences and goals. Don't get swayed by the allure of big jackpots; choose the game that aligns with your budget, risk tolerance, and playing style.

Next Up: We'll delve into the crucial aspect of responsible lottery play, equipping you with strategies to manage your finances and avoid the pitfalls of chasing unrealistic dreams.

State Lotteries vs. Multi-State Lotteries: Choosing Your Battleground

The American lottery landscape offers two main battlegrounds: **state lotteries** and **multi-state lotteries**. Each comes with its own set of pros and cons, and understanding these differences is vital before you choose your game.

State Lotteries:

- **Smaller Jackpots:**

While not offering the astronomical jackpots of their multi-state counterparts, state lotteries typically have smaller jackpots that are still significant prizes.

- **Higher Winning Odds:**

Because of the smaller jackpots and fewer players, the odds of winning smaller prizes tend to be higher in state lotteries compared to multi-state games.

- **Variety of Games:**

Many states offer diverse game options beyond the traditional Pick-n formats, including instant-win scratch-offs and games with unique features.

- **Local Support:**

A portion of state lottery proceeds often goes towards local programs and initiatives, potentially aligning with your social values.

Multi-State Lotteries:

- **Massive Jackpots:**

These games offer the potential for life-altering wealth, attracting millions of players and generating massive jackpots.

- **Lower Winning Odds:**

The sheer number of players translates to significantly lower odds of winning any prize, especially the jackpot.

- **Limited Game Selection:**

Multi-state lotteries typically offer a smaller selection of games compared to state lotteries, focusing primarily on the flagship jackpot games.

- **National Recognition:**

These games are widely known and advertised, creating a sense of excitement and anticipation.

Choosing Your Battleground:

- **Dream Chaser:**

If you have your sights set on the ultimate prize, multi-state lotteries might be tempting. However, remember the significantly lower odds and prioritize responsible play.

- **Value-Conscious Player:**

State lotteries offer a good balance of potential prize size and winning odds, potentially aligning with your risk tolerance and budget.

- **Local Supporter:**

If supporting local initiatives through lottery proceeds is important to you, research your state's lottery offerings and their impact.

Remember: There's no "one size fits all" answer. Consider your goals, risk tolerance, and budget when choosing your lottery battlefield. Don't get swayed solely by the allure of big jackpots; choose the game that aligns with your overall playing style and responsible financial practices.

Next Up: We'll delve into the crucial aspect of responsible lottery play, equipping you with strategies to manage your finances and avoid the pitfalls of chasing unrealistic dreams.

Chapter 3: Choosing Your Game (Continued) - Budget and Risk Tolerance

Now that you've explored the different game categories and battlegrounds, it's crucial to consider two key factors before diving into the lottery world: **your budget** and **your risk tolerance**.

Budget:
- **Set Limits:**
Determine a specific amount you're comfortable spending on lottery tickets per week, month, or year. Stick to this limit religiously, regardless of temptations or potential jackpots.
- **Prioritize Needs:**
Remember, lottery spending should never come at the expense of essential needs like rent, groceries, or healthcare. Ensure your basic needs are met before allocating any funds for lottery play.
- **Track Your Spending:**
Keep records of your lottery expenses to monitor your spending and ensure you're staying within your set budget.

Risk Tolerance:
- **Understand the Odds:**
Remember, the odds of winning the jackpot are incredibly low. Be prepared to accept the reality that you might not win anything, and approach lottery play as entertainment, not a guaranteed path to riches.
- **Match Your Playstyle:**
Choose games that align with your risk tolerance. If you're risk-averse, consider state lotteries with smaller jackpots but higher winning odds. If you're comfortable with higher risk, multi-state games might be tempting, but remember the significantly lower odds.
- **Don't Chase Losses:**
Resist the urge to throw more money at the lottery after losses. Remember, each ticket purchase is a new independent event, and past results don't influence future outcomes.

Balancing Budget and Risk:
- **Start Small:**

Begin with smaller ticket purchases and gradually increase if your budget allows, always prioritizing responsible spending.
- **Choose More Tickets over Bigger Bets:**

Opt for buying more tickets in games with higher winning odds instead of spending more on a single ticket for a bigger jackpot.
- **Consider Pools or Syndicates:**

Sharing the cost and winnings with others can be a way to potentially increase your chances while minimizing individual financial risk.

Remember: Responsible lottery play is crucial. Set realistic expectations, prioritize your financial well-being, and never chase losses. Treat lottery play as a form of entertainment, not a get-rich-quick scheme.

Next Up: We'll explore the concept of responsible lottery play in more detail, providing strategies and tips to ensure a safe and enjoyable experience.

Chapter 4: Responsible Lottery Play: Navigating the Game with Wisdom

The allure of the lottery is undeniable, but embarking on this journey requires a responsible approach. This chapter serves as your guide to navigating the lottery world with wisdom, ensuring your experience remains enjoyable and financially sound.

Setting Limits and Sticking to Them:
- **Budgeting is Key:**

Establish a dedicated budget for lottery play and adhere to it religiously. Remember, essentials like rent, food, and healthcare come first.

- **Track Your Spending:**

Maintain records of your lottery expenses to monitor your spending and avoid exceeding your budget.

- **Small Purchases, Big Impact:**

Opt for smaller, regular purchases instead of infrequent splurges on expensive tickets.

Avoiding Chasing Losses:
- **Remember the Odds:**

Lottery games are designed for the house to win. Accepting the reality of low winning odds is crucial.

- **Each Draw is Independent:**

Past results have no influence on future outcomes. Resist the urge to throw good money after bad in hopes of recouping losses.

- **Seek Help if Needed:**

If you find yourself struggling to control your spending or chasing losses, don't hesitate to seek professional help from gambling support organizations.

The Impact of Lottery Wins:
- **Plan for Taxes:**

Understand and prepare for the tax implications of lottery winnings. Consult a financial advisor to optimize your post-tax payout.

- **Seek Professional Guidance:**

Don't make hasty decisions. Seek advice from financial and legal professionals to manage your newfound wealth responsibly.

- **Live Within Your Means:**

Resist the temptation to splurge. Create a budget for managing your winnings wisely, prioritizing long-term financial security.

Beyond the Jackpot:
- **Enjoy the Game:**

Approach lottery play as entertainment, not a guaranteed path to riches. Focus on the fun and social aspects of the game.
- **Celebrate Small Wins:**

Appreciate and enjoy even small wins, reinforcing the entertainment value of the game.
- **Set Realistic Expectations:**

Remember, winning the jackpot is highly improbable. Manage your expectations and avoid chasing unrealistic dreams.

Remember: Responsible lottery play is not about winning, but about enjoying the experience within healthy boundaries. By prioritizing your financial well-being, setting realistic expectations, and seeking help if needed, you can ensure that your lottery journey remains positive and enriching.

Next Up: We'll delve into the exciting world of number selection strategies, exploring various methods to choose your lucky numbers and potentially increase your chances of winning.

Setting Limits and Sticking to Them: Your Guide to Responsible Lottery Play

The lottery can be a fun and exciting form of entertainment, but it's important to remember that it's a game of chance, and responsible play is crucial. Setting limits and sticking to them is the cornerstone of responsible lottery participation, ensuring you enjoy the game without jeopardizing your financial well-being. Here's a deeper dive into this key aspect:

Understanding Your Budget:
- **Know Your Numbers:**

Before you even consider buying a ticket, determine the amount you can comfortably afford to spend on the lottery per week, month, or year. This should be a small portion of your disposable income, not money needed for essentials or debt payments.

- **Prioritize Needs First:**

Remember, the lottery is entertainment, not a financial solution. Ensure all your essential needs like rent, groceries, and healthcare are met before allocating any funds for lottery play.

- **Track Your Spending:**

Keeping track of your lottery expenses is essential. Use a budgeting app, spreadsheet, or simply keep receipts to monitor your spending and stay within your set limits.

Setting Realistic Limits:
- **Start Small:**

Begin with smaller ticket purchases and gradually increase if your budget allows, always prioritizing responsible spending.

- **Consider Frequency:**

Decide how often you want to play. Daily play can quickly add up, so consider weekly or monthly purchases to manage your budget better.

- **Limit per Ticket:**

Set a limit on how much you're willing to spend on a single ticket. This helps avoid impulsively buying expensive tickets that exceed your budget.

Sticking to Your Limits:
- **Tell Yourself "No":**

Don't be afraid to say no to yourself or others who encourage you to spend more than you planned. Remember, you're in control of your spending.

- **Avoid Temptations:**

If you find yourself tempted to exceed your limits, walk away from the lottery retailer or online platform. Take a break and come back later with a clear head.

- **Seek Support:**

If you find it difficult to stick to your limits, don't hesitate to seek help from family, friends, or gambling support organizations.

Additional Tips:
- **Don't Chase Losses:**

Remember, each lottery draw is independent. Throwing more money at the game after losses will not increase your chances of winning and can lead to financial trouble.
- **Beware of "Hot" and "Cold" Numbers:**

These are just chance occurrences, and there's no scientific basis for them. Choose your numbers randomly or based on personal preference, but don't rely on these myths.
- **Consider Alternatives:**

If you find yourself struggling with impulse buying or exceeding your limits, explore alternative forms of entertainment that don't involve gambling.

Remember: Setting limits and sticking to them is crucial for responsible lottery play. By prioritizing your financial well-being, making informed decisions, and seeking help if needed, you can ensure a safe and enjoyable experience for yourself and those around you.

Next Up: We'll delve into the fascinating world of number selection strategies, exploring various methods to choose your lucky numbers and add a touch of excitement to your lottery journey.

Avoiding the Chasing Game: Breaking Free from Lottery Losses

The allure of the lottery lies in the possibility of sudden wealth, but the reality often involves chasing losses and potential financial hardship. This section empowers you to break free from this cycle and enjoy the game responsibly.

Understanding the Odds:
- **Odds Stacked Against You:**

Remember, the odds of winning the jackpot are astronomically low. Every draw is an independent event, so past losses have no bearing on future outcomes.

- **Temptation to Chase:**

The brain releases dopamine, a feel-good chemical, when we win, making us crave that feeling again. This can lead to chasing losses in an attempt to recapture the win, even though it's mathematically futile.

- **Accepting Reality:**

Embracing the low winning odds and treating the lottery as entertainment helps manage expectations and prevent chasing losses.

Breaking the Cycle:

- **Set Limits and Stick to Them:**

Establish a budget for lottery play and adhere to it religiously. Don't increase spending after losses; instead, remind yourself of your budget boundaries.

- **Focus on the Present:**

Forget past losses. Each draw is a new opportunity, and dwelling on the past can cloud your judgment and lead to impulsive decisions.

- **Seek Help if Needed:**

If you find yourself struggling to control your spending or chasing losses, don't hesitate to seek help from gambling support organizations or financial advisors.

Alternative Strategies:

- **Play for Fun, Not Riches:**

Approach the lottery as a form of light entertainment, not a guaranteed path to riches. Focus on the enjoyment of choosing numbers and the social aspects of playing with friends.

- **Celebrate Small Wins:**

Appreciate and celebrate even small wins, reinforcing the entertainment value of the game without getting caught up in chasing bigger prizes.

- **Explore Alternatives:**

Consider other recreational activities that don't involve gambling, such as hobbies, sports, or spending time with loved ones.

Remember:

- **Chasing losses is a common trap, but awareness is key to breaking free.**

- **Responsible lottery play prioritizes financial well-being and realistic expectations.**
- **Seek help if needed; you're not alone in this.**

Next Up: We'll delve into the exciting world of number selection strategies, exploring various methods to choose your lucky numbers and add a touch of excitement to your responsible lottery journey.

Winning the Lottery: Navigating the Impact on Your Life

While the odds are slim, winning the lottery can instantly change your life. But before you start dreaming of mansions and yachts, it's crucial to understand the potential impact on your personal and financial well-being. This section will guide you through navigating this life-altering event responsibly.

Immediate Reactions:
- **Emotional Rollercoaster:**

Expect a whirlwind of emotions, from disbelief and excitement to anxiety and fear. Seek support from trusted friends, family, or mental health professionals to navigate this emotional journey.
- **Media Frenzy:**

Winning big can attract unwanted attention from the media. Consider seeking legal and public relations advice to manage privacy and protect your safety.
- **Financial Decisions on Hold:**

Don't rush into any major financial decisions immediately. Take time to process the win, seek professional financial guidance, and develop a sound financial plan before making any significant changes.

Long-Term Impacts:
- **Lifestyle Changes:**

Winning can lead to significant lifestyle changes, impacting your relationships, work, and living situation. Communicate openly and honestly with loved ones and adjust to these changes gradually.
- **Financial Management:**

Wisely managing your newfound wealth is crucial. Invest with caution, avoid impulsive spending, and prioritize financial security for the long term.

- **Philanthropy:**

Consider using your wealth to give back to causes you care about. Philanthropy can be a fulfilling way to share your fortune and make a positive impact on the world.

Seeking Guidance:

- **Financial Advisor:**

A qualified financial advisor can help you develop a comprehensive wealth management plan, invest responsibly, and minimize tax liabilities.

- **Legal Counsel:**

An attorney can protect your legal interests, handle media inquiries, and ensure you comply with all legal requirements related to your winnings.

- **Tax Consultant:**

Understanding and preparing for the tax implications of your win is crucial. Seek guidance from a tax professional to ensure you comply with all tax regulations.

Remember:

- Winning the lottery is a life-changing event, but it comes with its own set of challenges.
- Prioritizing responsible financial management, seeking professional guidance, and navigating emotional changes are key to making the most of your win.
- Don't let your newfound wealth define you. Stay grounded, maintain healthy relationships, and use your fortune to create a fulfilling and meaningful life.

Next Up: We'll explore the exciting world of number selection strategies, adding a touch of fun and excitement to your responsible lottery journey.

Part 2: Number Selection Strategies: Adding a Spark to Your Responsible Play

While responsible lottery play prioritizes financial well-being and realistic expectations, there's still room for a touch of fun! Let's explore various number selection strategies, adding a layer of excitement to your lottery journey without compromising responsibility.

Remember: These strategies don't guarantee a win, but they can make your playing experience more engaging and personalize your participation.

Random Selection:
- **The Classic Approach:**
This simple method involves choosing numbers randomly, relying solely on chance. It's quick, easy, and avoids biases.
- **Quick Picks:**
Utilize the random selection feature offered by lottery retailers, letting fate choose your numbers.

Personalized Numbers:
- **Birthdays, Anniversaries, Lucky Numbers:**
Incorporate personally significant dates or numbers that hold special meaning for you, adding a sentimental touch.
- **Numerology:**
Explore number meanings and choose numbers based on their symbolic associations, adding a layer of mysticism.

Pattern-Based Strategies:
- **Wheeling:**
This systematic method involves selecting more numbers than usual, covering specific number combinations and potentially increasing your chances of winning smaller prizes. However, it requires purchasing multiple tickets, so be mindful of your budget.
- **Conditional Picking:**
Choose specific numbers based on predetermined criteria, like picking numbers that haven't appeared in a certain number of draws or avoiding consecutive numbers.

Pool Play and Syndicates:
- **Teamwork Makes the Dream Work:**

Join forces with friends, family, or colleagues to purchase multiple tickets, sharing the cost and potentially increasing your chances of winning. Establish clear rules and agreements beforehand to ensure smooth collaboration.

Remember:
- **There's no "magic formula" for winning the lottery.** All selection methods rely on chance.
- **Focus on the fun and social aspects of playing.** Enjoy the process of choosing numbers and sharing the experience with others.
- **Stay within your budget and stick to your limits.** Don't let your chosen strategy lead to irresponsible spending.

Bonus Tip: Regardless of your chosen strategy, keep your numbers organized and track your tickets to avoid missing out on potential wins!

Next Up: We'll conclude with some final words of wisdom and encouragement, leaving you empowered to embark on your responsible lottery journey with confidence and a touch of fun.

Chapter 5: Random Number Selection - Embracing Chance and Enjoying the Ride

While the allure of the lottery lies in the dream of life-altering wealth, it's crucial to approach it with realistic expectations and responsible practices. This final chapter serves as a reminder to prioritize enjoyment, manage your finances wisely, and embrace the element of chance that makes the lottery experience unique.

Randomness: The Heart of the Game:

Remember, lottery draws are based entirely on random chance. No number selection strategy, regardless of its complexity, can guarantee a win. Embrace this element of chance and focus on enjoying the process of choosing your numbers and participating in the draw.

Responsible Play: Your Guiding Light:

Throughout this journey, we've emphasized the importance of responsible lottery play. Set limits, stick to your budget, and avoid chasing losses. Remember, the lottery is entertainment, not a financial solution.

Beyond the Jackpot:

Winning the jackpot is a dream, but it's not the only way to enjoy the lottery. Celebrate even small wins, appreciate the social aspects of playing with friends or family, and focus on the fun and excitement of the draw.

Farewell and Best Wishes:

As you embark on your lottery journey, remember the key takeaways:

- **Prioritize responsible play:**
Set limits, stick to your budget, and seek help if needed.
- **Embrace the element of chance:**
Enjoy the excitement of random selection without chasing unrealistic dreams.
- **Focus on the fun:**
Celebrate small wins, connect with others, and treat the lottery as a form of entertainment.

May your lottery experience be filled with fun, responsible choices, and a touch of luck!

Quick Picks: Pros and Cons for Your Lottery Journey

Quick picks, where the lottery system randomly selects your numbers, are a popular option for many players. But before you hit the "Quick Pick" button, let's weigh the pros and cons to see if it's the right choice for you:

Pros:

- **Convenience:**

It's the fastest and easiest way to play. No need to brainstorm or spend time picking individual numbers.

- **Avoids Biases:**

Eliminates personal biases that might lead you to choose predictable or repetitive numbers.

- **Potential for Surprise:**

You might just stumble upon a winning combination you wouldn't have picked yourself!

- **Social Play:**

You can easily share Quick Picks with friends or colleagues for a fun group activity.

Cons:

- **Lower Odds:**

By not choosing your own numbers, you potentially miss out on "lucky" numbers or specific combinations you favor.

- **Less Personalization:**

You lose the sentimentality and fun of choosing numbers with personal meaning.

- **Budget Concerns:**

Quick Picks often involve buying multiple tickets, which can add up quickly and exceed your budget.

- **No Control:**

You completely surrender control over your number selection, which might be less exciting for some players.

Ultimately, the decision to use Quick Picks depends on your preferences and playing style:

- **Choose Quick Picks if:**

You prioritize convenience and speed, want to avoid biases, or enjoy the element of surprise.

- **Avoid Quick Picks if:**

You prefer personalized number selection, want more control over your choices, or have a limited budget.

Remember:

- Responsible play is key, regardless of your selection method. Set limits, stick to your budget, and treat the lottery as entertainment.

- Whether you choose Quick Picks or select your own numbers, enjoy the process and good luck!

Random Number Generators and Tools: A Balancing Act between Fun and Responsibility

While random number generators (RNGs) and tools can add a layer of fun and personalization to your lottery experience, it's crucial to approach them with caution and maintain responsible playing practices. Here's a breakdown of their potential benefits and drawbacks:

Benefits:

- **Convenience:**

RNGs and tools can quickly generate numerous number combinations, saving you time and effort compared to manual selection.

- **Personalization:**

Some tools allow you to filter or exclude numbers based on your preferences, offering a level of customization beyond Quick Picks.

- **Exploration:**

You can experiment with different strategies and number combinations, potentially leading to new insights or lucky discoveries.

- **Sharing and Fun:**

RNGs can be a fun way to generate numbers with friends or family, adding a social element to the playing experience.

Drawbacks:
- **Misplaced Trust:**

RNGs and tools **don't** increase your chances of winning. They simply generate random combinations, and relying on them might lead to unrealistic expectations.
- **Budget Concerns:**

Some tools offer paid features or encourage purchasing multiple tickets based on their suggestions, potentially exceeding your budget.
- **Over-reliance:**

Avoid becoming overly reliant on RNGs for number selection. Remember, the element of chance and personal choice is part of the lottery experience.
- **Addiction Potential:**

Be mindful of the potential for excessive use of these tools, which could lead to impulsive spending or neglecting other responsibilities.

Responsible Play Tips:
- **Set limits:**

Determine your budget and stick to it, regardless of what RNGs or tools suggest.
- **Use them for fun:**

Treat RNGs as a way to explore different combinations, not a guaranteed path to winning.
- **Maintain control:**

Don't let tools dictate your choices entirely. Maintain some element of personal selection and avoid relying solely on them.
- **Seek help if needed:**

If you find yourself struggling with responsible play or exceeding your limits, don't hesitate to seek help from gambling support organizations.

Remember: RNGs and tools can be fun additions to your lottery journey, but prioritize responsible play, manage your budget wisely, and enjoy the process without relying on them for unrealistic expectations.

Debunking the Myth: "Hot" and "Cold" Numbers in the Lottery

The allure of the lottery often leads players to chase strategies that promises higher winning odds. One such persistent belief is the concept of "hot" and "cold" numbers, where "hot" numbers are those that have appeared frequently in recent draws and "cold" numbers are those that haven't shown up in a while.

However, it's crucial to understand that **the myth of "hot" and "cold" numbers is just that - a myth.** Here's why:

Randomness Reigns Supreme:

Lottery draws are designed to be completely random. Each number has an equal probability of being drawn in any given draw, regardless of its past appearances. Past results have **absolutely no bearing** on future outcomes.

False Correlations:

The human brain is wired to seek patterns and connections, even where none exist. Observing a string of draws where certain numbers haven't appeared might create the illusion that they're "due" to come up soon, but this is simply a cognitive bias and has no basis in reality.

The Cost of Chasing Ghosts:

Focusing on "hot" and "cold" numbers can lead to irresponsible play. Players might spend more money on tickets chasing these elusive numbers, neglecting their budget and potentially exceeding their limits.

Embrace the Fun, Not False Hopes:

Instead of chasing myths, remember that the lottery is primarily about entertainment. Enjoy the process of choosing your numbers, participating in the draw, and sharing the experience with others.

Here are some tips for responsible and enjoyable lottery play:

- Set and stick to a budget.
- Choose numbers that you find meaningful or fun, not based on myths.
- Celebrate small wins and focus on the enjoyment of the game.
- Remember that winning the jackpot is highly improbable.
- Seek help if you find yourself struggling with responsible play.

By understanding the myth of "hot" and "cold" numbers and prioritizing responsible practices, you can ensure that your lottery experience remains fun, engaging, and financially sound.

Chapter 6: Pattern-Based Number Selection: Exploring Strategies with Caution

In the realm of lottery play, where chance reigns supreme, some players seek strategies beyond random selection. Pattern-based number selection methods offer a structured approach, potentially increasing the chances of winning smaller prizes. However, it's crucial to understand their limitations and prioritize responsible play.

Common Pattern-Based Strategies:
- **Wheeling:**

This systematic approach involves selecting more numbers than usual, covering specific number combinations. While it increases your chances of winning smaller prizes if some of your numbers match, it also requires purchasing multiple tickets, potentially exceeding your budget.
- **Conditional Picking:**

This strategy involves choosing numbers based on predetermined criteria, like picking numbers that haven't appeared in a certain number of draws or avoiding consecutive numbers. While it can be fun and personalized, it doesn't guarantee any advantage and might limit your number choices.
- **Sum and Difference Methods:**

These involve calculations based on the sum or difference of past winning numbers. However, remember that past results have no bearing on future outcomes, making these methods purely theoretical and offering no real advantage.

Understanding the Limitations:
- **No Guaranteed Wins:**

It's important to remember that **no pattern-based strategy can guarantee a win**. Lottery draws are random, and all numbers have an equal chance of being drawn, regardless of past patterns.
- **Increased Cost:**

Some strategies, like wheeling, require purchasing multiple tickets, which can quickly add up and exceed your budget. Always prioritize responsible spending and stick to your limits.

- **Focus on Entertainment:**

Treat these strategies as a fun way to personalize your experience, not a guaranteed path to riches. Enjoy the process of choosing your numbers and the excitement of the draw.

Responsible Play Tips:
- **Set a budget and stick to it.**

Don't let any strategy tempt you to spend more than you can afford.
- **Combine patterns with random selection.**

Don't rely solely on patterns; incorporate some random numbers for added personalization and fun.
- **Celebrate small wins.**

Focus on the enjoyment of the game and appreciate even small winnings.
- **Seek help if needed.**

If you find yourself struggling with responsible play or exceeding your limits, don't hesitate to seek help from gambling support organizations.

Remember: Pattern-based strategies can add a layer of interest to your lottery experience, but they should be approached with caution and never replace responsible play. Enjoy the game, manage your finances wisely, and prioritize fun over unrealistic expectations.

Next Up: We'll conclude with some final words of wisdom and encouragement, leaving you empowered to embark on your responsible lottery journey with confidence and a touch of fun.

Identifying and Analyzing Past Winning Numbers: A Balanced Perspective

The allure of the lottery often leads players to seek patterns and insights from past winning numbers, hoping to gain an advantage. While analyzing historical data can be interesting and potentially spark strategies, it's crucial to approach it with **realistic expectations and responsible play principles**.

Why Past Numbers Don't Predict the Future:

Lottery draws are designed to be **completely random**. Each number has an equal probability of being drawn in any given draw, regardless of how many times it has appeared (or not appeared) in the past. Analyzing past results is like trying to predict the roll of a fair die based on previous rolls; it simply doesn't work.

Potential Biases and Misconceptions:
- ### Clustering Illusion:
Observing a string of draws where certain numbers haven't appeared might create the illusion that they're "due" to come up soon. This is just **cognitive bias**, and there's no evidence to support it.
- ### Overfitting and Confirmation Bias:
Focusing on patterns that align with your existing beliefs (confirmation bias) can lead to overfitting, where you identify patterns that might not actually exist in the larger dataset.
- ### Ignoring Sample Size:
Analyzing a small sample of past draws might lead to inaccurate conclusions. Consider a larger dataset for more representative results, but remember, randomness still prevails.

Responsible Play and Enjoyment:
Instead of chasing elusive patterns, remember these key points for responsible and enjoyable lottery play:
- Focus on entertainment, not riches.
- Set a budget and stick to it.
- Choose numbers that you find meaningful or fun.
- Celebrate small wins.
- Don't chase losses.
- Seek help if you find yourself struggling with responsible play.

Alternatives to Past Number Analysis:
- ### Random selection:
Embrace the element of chance and choose numbers randomly.
- ### Personalized choices:
Pick numbers with personal significance, like birthdays or anniversaries.
- ### Pattern-based strategies:
Use them for fun, but remember they don't guarantee wins.

Remember: While analyzing past numbers can be a thought experiment, it shouldn't be your primary strategy. Prioritize responsible play, manage your finances wisely, and enjoy the lottery for what it is: a fun and unpredictable game of chance.

Using mathematical formulas and sequences

While the desire to gain an edge in the lottery is understandable, using mathematical formulas and sequences to predict winning numbers is **futile and can lead to irresponsible play.** Here's why:

The Flawed Premise:

- **Lottery draws are completely random.**

Each number has an equal chance of being drawn, regardless of past results or calculations. No formula or sequence can predict this randomness.

- **Mathematical patterns don't translate to lottery outcomes.**

Applying mathematical concepts like probability distribution or Fibonacci sequences to lottery numbers is a misuse of these concepts. They don't account for the inherent randomness of the draws.

Potential Harms:

- **Misplaced Trust:**

Relying on formulas or sequences might lead to unrealistic expectations and excessive spending, potentially exceeding your budget and jeopardizing your financial well-being.

- **Ignoring Responsible Play:**

Focusing on complex calculations can distract you from the core principles of responsible lottery play, like setting limits and prioritizing entertainment over winning.

- **Perpetuating Myths:**

The belief that formulas can predict lottery outcomes is a persistent myth that can mislead players and encourage irresponsible practices.

Alternatives for Enjoyable Play:

- **Random Selection:**

Embrace the element of chance and choose numbers randomly for a fun and unpredictable experience.

- **Personalized Choices:**

Pick numbers with personal significance, like birthdays or anniversaries, adding a sentimental touch.

- **Pattern-Based Strategies:**

Use them for fun and personalization, but remember they don't guarantee wins.

- **Focus on the Entertainment:**

Enjoy the social aspects of playing with friends, the excitement of the draw, and celebrating even small wins.

Remember:

- **Responsible play is paramount.**

Set limits, stick to your budget, and prioritize your financial well-being.

- **Lottery draws are random.**

No formula or sequence can overcome this fundamental principle.

- **Enjoy the game for what it is.**

Focus on the fun and social aspects, not unrealistic expectations of winning.

By understanding the limitations of mathematical formulas and sequences and embracing responsible play practices, you can ensure that your lottery experience remains enjoyable and financially sound.

Understanding the Limitations of Patterns in Lottery Play: Enjoying the Game Responsibly

While searching for patterns in lottery results can be tempting, it's crucial to understand their limitations and approach them strategically to avoid falling into pitfalls. Here's a breakdown of the key points:

Why Patterns Don't Guarantee Wins:

- **Randomness Reigns Supreme:**

Lottery draws are designed to be completely random. Each number has an equal chance of being drawn, regardless of past occurrences. Past patterns, no matter how compelling they seem, offer no predictive power for future outcomes.

- **Confirmation Bias and Overfitting:**

Our brains are wired to seek patterns, even where none exist. Focusing on patterns that align with our existing beliefs (confirmation bias) can lead to overfitting, where we identify patterns that might not be statistically significant in the larger dataset.

- **Sample Size Matters:**

Analyzing a small sample of past draws can lead to inaccurate conclusions. While looking at a larger dataset is helpful, remember, randomness still prevails.

Responsible Play Tips:
- **Focus on Enjoyment, Not Riches:**

Treat the lottery as a form of entertainment, not a guaranteed path to wealth. Set realistic expectations and prioritize fun over potential winnings.
- **Stick to Your Budget:**

Allocate a small portion of your disposable income for lottery play and never exceed your limits. Responsible spending is key to enjoying the game without jeopardizing your financial well-being.
- **Choose Numbers You Like:**

Pick numbers that hold personal meaning or simply appeal to you. This way, you'll enjoy the process of choosing and have a sentimental connection to your ticket, regardless of the outcome.
- **Celebrate Small Wins:**

Appreciate and celebrate even small winnings, reinforcing the fun aspect of the game and avoiding the disappointment of chasing larger prizes.

Alternatives to Pattern-Based Strategies:
- **Embrace Randomness:**

Choose numbers randomly for a fun and unpredictable experience.
- **Combine Methods:**

Incorporate some random numbers with personalized choices or a limited pattern-based approach for a bit of both worlds.
- **Enjoy the Social Aspect:**

Play with friends or family, share the excitement of the draw, and focus on the social interaction and connection.

Remember:
- **Patterns are interesting, but they don't predict the future.**
- **Responsible play is crucial.** Set limits, prioritize fun, and never chase losses.
- **The lottery is a game of chance.** Enjoy the ride without unrealistic expectations.

By understanding the limitations of patterns and adopting responsible play practices, you can ensure that your lottery experience remains enjoyable and financially sound.

Chapter 7: Wheeling and Lottery Pools: Navigating Strategies with Responsibility

As you delve deeper into the world of lottery play, you might encounter two intriguing strategies: wheeling and lottery pools. While both can offer unique advantages, it's crucial to understand their nuances and approach them with responsible play practices in mind.

Wheeling: Covering More Ground, But at a Cost

Wheeling involves selecting more numbers than usual and strategically combining them into multiple tickets, ensuring you win a smaller prize if a certain number of your chosen numbers match the drawn ones.

Benefits:
- **Increases chances of winning smaller prizes:**
By covering more number combinations, you have a higher chance of winning something, even if it's not the jackpot.
- **Can be customized:**
You can choose the level of coverage and number of tickets based on your budget and preferences.

Drawbacks:
- **Requires multiple tickets:**
This can significantly increase your spending, potentially exceeding your budget if not carefully planned.
- **Complexity:**
Wheeling can be confusing, especially for beginners. Understanding the different wheeling systems and their implications is crucial.
- **No guarantee of winning:**
Even with wheeling, winning the jackpot or larger prizes remains highly improbable.

Lottery Pools: Sharing the Cost and the Joy

Lottery pools involve joining forces with friends, family, or colleagues to purchase multiple tickets together, sharing the cost and potentially increasing your chances of winning.

Benefits:
- **Reduced individual cost:**

Sharing the ticket cost allows you to participate in more draws or buy more tickets without exceeding your budget.
- **Social aspect:**

Playing with others can add a fun and collaborative element to the lottery experience.
- **Increased potential winnings:**

If your pool wins, the payout is shared among members, potentially leading to larger individual rewards.

Drawbacks:
- **Trust and communication:**

Establishing clear rules and communication within the pool is crucial to avoid disputes and ensure everyone is on the same page.
- **Prize sharing:**

Be prepared to share any winnings according to the agreed-upon terms, even if your individual contribution was smaller.
- **Tax implications:**

Understand the tax implications of winning as part of a pool to avoid surprises later.

Responsible Play Tips for Both Strategies:
- **Set a budget and stick to it:**

Don't let wheeling or pool participation tempt you to exceed your spending limits.
- **Do the math:**

Calculate the cost involved in wheeling or pool participation before committing.
- **Communicate clearly:**

If joining a pool, establish clear rules and expectations regarding contributions, payouts, and decision-making.
- **Focus on the fun:**

Remember, the lottery is primarily about entertainment. Enjoy the social aspects and the excitement of the draw, regardless of the outcome.

Remember: Both wheeling and lottery pools can be fun and engaging strategies, but prioritize responsible play and manage your finances wisely. Enjoy the journey, prioritize fun over unrealistic expectations, and never let these strategies compromise your financial well-being.

Next Up: We'll conclude with some final words of wisdom and encouragement, leaving you empowered to embark on your responsible lottery journey with confidence and a touch of fun.

Increasing your odds by covering more numbers

While it's true that covering more numbers in the lottery **can** increase your chances of winning smaller prizes, it's important to understand the nuances and potential drawbacks before diving in. Here's a breakdown:

Does covering more numbers guarantee a win?

No, unfortunately, covering more numbers **does not guarantee** a win in the lottery. Every number has an equal chance of being drawn, regardless of how many other numbers you choose. While selecting more numbers increases your chances of matching some of the drawn numbers, it doesn't guarantee you'll match the specific combination needed for the jackpot or even larger prizes.

Strategies for covering more numbers:
- **Wheeling:**

This involves strategically selecting sets of numbers and combining them into multiple tickets, ensuring you win a smaller prize if a certain number of your choices match the drawn ones. While it increases coverage, it also requires buying more tickets, which can significantly impact your budget.

- **Lottery pools:**

Joining forces with others to purchase multiple tickets together can spread the cost and increase your coverage, but remember to share any winnings according to the agreed-upon terms.

Important considerations:
- **Cost:**

Covering more numbers often involves spending more money. Ensure these strategies fit your budget and don't lead to irresponsible spending.
- **Complexity:**

Wheeling can be confusing, especially for beginners. Understand the different systems and their implications before using them.
- **Limited impact:**

Even with extensive coverage, the odds of winning the jackpot or larger prizes remain very low.

Alternatives to consider:
- **Random selection:**

Embrace the element of chance and choose numbers randomly for a fun and unpredictable experience.
- **Personalized choices:**

Pick numbers with personal meaning or that simply appeal to you, adding a sentimental touch to your participation.
- **Focus on the fun:**

Remember, the lottery is primarily about entertainment. Enjoy the social aspects, the excitement of the draw, and celebrating even small wins.

Remember:

Responsible play is crucial. Set limits, stick to your budget, and prioritize fun over unrealistic expectations. While covering more numbers can be a strategy, manage your finances wisely and never let it compromise your financial well-being.

I hope this clarifies the potential benefits and drawbacks of covering more numbers in the lottery. Play responsibly and enjoy the journey

Forming syndicates and sharing winnings

Forming syndicates and sharing winnings in the lottery can be a fun and social way to participate, but it's crucial to approach it with clear communication, responsible play, and legal considerations in mind. Here's a breakdown of the key points:

Benefits:

- **Reduced cost:**

Sharing the cost of tickets amongst members can make participating in larger draws or buying more tickets more affordable for everyone.

- **Increased odds:**

By pooling resources and covering more numbers, you can potentially increase your chances of winning smaller prizes.

- **Social aspect:**

Playing with friends, family, or colleagues can add a fun and collaborative element to the experience.

- **Shared celebration:**

Winning as a group can be even more exciting and rewarding, shared amongst everyone who contributed.

Drawbacks:

Trust and communication:

Establishing clear rules and communicating openly about expectations, contributions, and prize sharing is crucial to avoid disputes later.

- **Legal implications:**

Depending on your location, there might be legal requirements or tax implications associated with winning as a syndicate. Be sure to research and comply with all relevant regulations.

- **Potential for conflict:**

Disagreements about how to spend winnings or manage the syndicate can arise. Clear communication and established rules can help mitigate this.

- **Smaller individual share:**

While you share the cost, you also share the winnings, potentially resulting in a smaller individual payout compared to winning solo.

Tips for responsible syndicate play:

- **Set clear rules and agreements:**

Establish a written agreement outlining everyone's contributions, responsibilities, and how winnings will be shared and distributed.

- **Choose trustworthy members:**

Only include people you trust and who are committed to responsible play.

- **Communicate openly:**

Maintain open communication throughout the process, addressing any concerns or questions promptly.

- **Manage finances wisely:**

Set a budget for your syndicate participation and stick to it. Don't let it lead to overspending.

- **Understand legal requirements:**

Research any legal or tax implications associated with winning as a syndicate in your jurisdiction.

Remember:

- Syndicates can be fun, but prioritize responsible play.
- Clear communication and legal awareness are key.
- Focus on the fun and social aspects, not just the potential winnings.

By approaching syndicate formation and winnings responsibly, you can ensure a positive and enjoyable experience for everyone involved.

The legal and financial considerations of pools

While lottery pools offer a chance to share the cost and excitement of the game, it's crucial to navigate the legal and financial considerations before diving in. Here's a breakdown of key points to remember:

Legal Aspects:

Formation: Depending on your location, there might be specific legal requirements for forming a lottery pool. Research your local laws and regulations to ensure compliance.

- **Agreements:**

A written agreement outlining contributions, prize distribution, and dispute resolution is essential to protect everyone involved. Consult a lawyer to create a legally sound document.

- **Tax Implications:**

Winnings from a lottery pool might be subject to different tax regulations than individual winnings. Understand your tax obligations and ensure proper reporting.

- **Responsible Gaming:**

Be aware of responsible gaming regulations in your area and ensure your pool adheres to them.

Financial Considerations:
- **Budgeting:**

Set a clear budget for your pool participation and stick to it. Avoid exceeding individual limits or putting anyone in financial strain.
- **Cost Sharing:**

Determine a fair and transparent method for sharing the cost of tickets based on individual contributions or agreed-upon percentages.
- **Winnings Distribution:**

Establish a clear and pre-determined plan for distributing any winnings, taking into account contributions and agreed-upon shares.
- **Record Keeping:**

Maintain accurate records of contributions, purchases, and winnings for transparency and potential tax purposes.

Additional Tips:
- **Choose trustworthy members:**

Only include people you trust and who understand and respect the agreed-upon rules and financial implications.
- **Communicate openly:**

Maintain open communication throughout the process, addressing any concerns or questions promptly.
- **Seek professional guidance:**

Consult a lawyer or financial advisor if you have complex legal or financial questions regarding your pool.

Remember:
- **Responsible play is paramount.**

Prioritize financial well-being and avoid exceeding your limits.
- **Legal compliance is crucial.**

Understand and follow all relevant regulations to avoid legal issues.
- **Clear communication and agreements are essential.**

Ensure everyone involved is on the same page to prevent future disputes.

By navigating the legal and financial considerations responsibly and prioritizing clear communication, you can create a fun and rewarding lottery pool experience for everyone involved.

Part 3: Advanced Strategies and Techniques

Embark on the Lottery Adventure: Unveiling Advanced Strategies and Techniques!

Congratulations, fellow adventurer! You've mastered the basics of navigating the exciting world of lottery play. Now, prepare to delve deeper into a treasure trove of advanced strategies and techniques that can enhance your enjoyment and potentially increase your chances of striking gold (or at least striking silver!).

But remember, dear explorer, responsible play remains our guiding star. This journey isn't about chasing unrealistic riches, but about unlocking the hidden potential of the game with a healthy dose of fun and responsible choices.

What awaits you in this thrilling Part 3?

- **Number Selection Mastery:**

We'll explore diverse approaches beyond random picks, from the strategic world of wheeling to the collaborative spirit of lottery pools. Dive into pattern analysis, mathematical formulas (used responsibly, of course!), and other intriguing methods to personalize your number selection process.

- **Unveiling the Myths:**

We'll shed light on common misconceptions like "hot" and "cold" numbers, revealing the truth behind these lottery legends and empowering you to make informed decisions based on reality, not wishful thinking.

- **Syndicates and Shared Fortune:**

Discover the joys and legalities of forming lottery syndicates with friends, family, or colleagues. Learn how to navigate cost-sharing, prize distribution, and legal considerations to ensure a harmonious and rewarding syndicate experience.

- **Beyond the Jackpot:**

Remember, the lottery is more than just the jackpot dream! We'll explore strategies to maximize your enjoyment by celebrating small wins, focusing on the social aspects of the game, and setting realistic expectations.

Remember, adventurer:

- **Responsible play is the ultimate prize.**

Set limits, stick to your budget, and prioritize fun over unrealistic expectations.

- **Knowledge is power.**

This chapter equips you with diverse strategies, but remember, responsible play and a touch of luck are your true companions.

- **Enjoy the journey!**

Embrace the excitement of the draw, share the experience with loved ones, and celebrate every win, big or small.

So, are you ready to embark on this exciting exploration of advanced lottery strategies and techniques? Buckle up, adventurer, and let's begin!

Chapter 8: Demystifying the Maze: Lottery Software and Analysis Tools

In the ever-evolving world of lottery play, technology beckons with a plethora of software and analysis tools, promising to unlock the secrets to winning. But before venturing into this digital landscape, let's approach it with a discerning eye and a firm grasp of responsible play principles.

Exploring the Toolbox:
- **Random Number Generators (RNGs):**
These tools churn out random number combinations, offering a quick and convenient way to choose your numbers. While convenient, remember, randomness is the core of the lottery, and RNGs don't guarantee any advantage.
- **Wheeling Software:**
These programs automate the complex calculations involved in wheeling strategies, helping you cover more number combinations without manually generating tickets. However, understand the cost implications and choose responsible wheeling options.
- **Pattern Analysis Tools:**
These programs analyze past draws, identifying patterns or trends. While intriguing, remember that past results have no bearing on future outcomes. Use these tools for entertainment, not as predictors.
- **Lottery Syndicates Apps:**
These platforms facilitate forming and managing lottery syndicates online, streamlining communication and prize distribution. Remember, clear communication and responsible financial practices are still crucial.

The Discerning Player's Guide:
- **Focus on entertainment, not riches.**
Don't invest heavily in software based on unrealistic expectations. Use them for fun, not as guaranteed pathways to wealth.
- **Understand the limitations.**
These tools are not magic wands. They can't predict winning numbers or overcome the inherent randomness of the lottery.

- **Beware of hidden costs.**

Some software or apps might have subscription fees or in-app purchases. Be mindful of your budget and avoid overspending.

- **Stick to responsible play principles.**

Don't let the excitement of tools tempt you to exceed your budget or engage in risky play.

Alternatives to Consider:

- **Embrace random selection:**

Choose numbers randomly for a fun and unpredictable experience.

- **Personalize your choices:**

Pick numbers with personal meaning, adding a sentimental touch to your participation.

- **Focus on the social aspects:**

Play with friends or family, share the excitement of the draw, and enjoy the shared experience.

Remember:

- **Responsible play is paramount.**

Prioritize your financial well-being and avoid relying solely on software or tools.

- **Enjoy the process.**

The lottery is a game of chance, so focus on the fun and excitement, not just the potential winnings.

- **Use tools responsibly.**

If you choose to use them, do so with a clear understanding of their limitations and prioritize responsible play practices.

By approaching lottery software and analysis tools with a discerning eye and prioritizing responsible play, you can ensure that your journey through this digital landscape remains enjoyable and financially sound.

Evaluating Software Claims and Effectiveness: A Guide for Discerning Lottery Players

The allure of winning big draws players towards various lottery software and analysis tools, each promising to unlock the secrets to success. But before investing your time and money, it's crucial to approach these claims with a critical eye and a firm grasp of responsible play principles.

Evaluating Software Claims:
- **Beware of exaggerated promises:**

Look for red flags like guarantees of wins or claims of "cracking the code." Remember, lottery draws are completely random, and no software can predict future outcomes.
- **Understand the limitations:**

Most software focuses on number selection or pattern analysis. While these can be fun tools, they don't offer any real advantage over random selection.
- **Research the company and product:**

Check the reputation of the software developer, read reviews from independent sources, and understand the specific features and limitations of the tool before purchasing.

Assessing Effectiveness:
- **Focus on entertainment value:**

If the software enhances your enjoyment of the lottery experience through features like random number generation or personalized statistics, it might be worth considering.
- **Don't expect miracles:**

Don't base your purchase decision on testimonials or anecdotal evidence of wins. Remember, winning is based on chance, and individual experiences don't guarantee future results.
- **Compare features and costs:**

Compare different software options, considering features, pricing models, and any potential hidden costs like subscriptions or in-app purchases.

Responsible Play Tips:
- **Set a budget for software and stick to it.**

Don't let the excitement of tools tempt you to overspend.
- **Don't rely solely on software for number selection:**

Use it for fun and personalization, but always incorporate random choices or personal preferences.
- **Focus on realistic expectations:** Remember, the lottery is a game of chance, and winning the jackpot is highly improbable. Enjoy the process and celebrate small wins.

Alternatives to Consider:
- **Embrace random selection:**
Choose numbers randomly for a fun and unpredictable experience.
- **Personalize your choices:** Pick numbers with personal meaning, adding a sentimental touch to your participation.
- **Focus on the social aspects:**
Play with friends or family, share the excitement of the draw, and enjoy the shared experience.

Remember:
- **Responsible play is paramount.**
Prioritize your financial well-being and avoid relying solely on software or tools to win.
- **Enjoy the process.**
The lottery is a game of chance, so focus on the fun and excitement, not just the potential winnings.
- **Use software responsibly.**
If you choose to use them, do so with a clear understanding of their limitations and prioritize responsible play practices.

By approaching lottery software and analysis tools with a discerning eye and prioritizing responsible play, you can ensure that your journey through this digital landscape remains enjoyable and financially sound.

Data Analysis and the Lottery: Separating Fact from Fiction
The allure of using data analysis to predict winning lottery numbers is understandable. However, it's crucial to understand that **data analysis cannot guarantee wins** in a game based entirely on randomness. While analyzing past data can be an interesting exercise, it's important to approach it with **realistic expectations and responsible play principles**.

Why Data Analysis Doesn't Predict Winners:
- **Lottery draws are completely random:**
Each number has an equal chance of being drawn, regardless of past results. Analyzing past patterns or trends offers no true insight into future outcomes.

- **Data analysis can be misleading:**

Focusing on specific patterns or trends can lead to overfitting, where you identify patterns that might not actually exist in the larger dataset.

- **Limited data:**

Analyzing a small sample of past draws might lead to inaccurate conclusions. While considering a larger dataset is helpful, remember, randomness still prevails.

Responsible Play and Enjoyment:

Instead of chasing elusive patterns, remember these key points for responsible and enjoyable lottery play:

- Focus on entertainment, not riches.
- Set a budget and stick to it.
- Choose numbers that you find meaningful or fun.
- Celebrate small wins.
- Don't chase losses.
- Seek help if you find yourself struggling with responsible play.

Alternatives to Data Analysis:

- **Random selection:**

Embrace the element of chance and choose numbers randomly for a fun and unpredictable experience.

- **Personalized choices:**

Pick numbers with personal significance, like birthdays or anniversaries.

- **Pattern-based strategies:**

Use them for fun, but remember they don't guarantee wins.

Remember :

- **Responsible play is paramount.**

Prioritize your financial well-being and manage your finances wisely.

- **Data analysis in the lottery context has limitations.**

Don't rely on it to predict winners.

- **Enjoy the game for what it is.**

Focus on the fun and social aspects, not unrealistic expectations of winning.

By understanding the limitations of data analysis and embracing responsible play practices, you can ensure that your lottery experience remains enjoyable and financially sound.

Additionally:

- If you're interested in data analysis for other purposes, it can be a valuable tool in various fields. However, it's crucial to understand its limitations and ethical considerations in each context.

- Remember, responsible play is not just about avoiding data analysis misuse. It encompasses setting limits, managing budgets, and prioritizing entertainment over unrealistic expectations.

The Importance of Responsible Software Use in Lottery Play: A Guide for Savvy Players

While software and analysis tools can add an interesting layer to lottery play, it's crucial to approach them with responsible practices and realistic expectations. Here's why:

Understanding the Risks:

- **Overspending:**

Some software might encourage excessive spending through features like automated ticket purchases or subscription fees. Always stick to your budget and avoid exceeding your financial limits.

- **Misleading Claims:**

Beware of software promising guaranteed wins or claiming to "crack the code." Lottery draws are completely random, and no software can predict future outcomes.

- **Unrealistic Expectations:**

Relying solely on software can lead to disappointment and financial strain if you base your hopes on unrealistic expectations of winning big.

Promoting Responsible Play:

- **Focus on Entertainment:**

Treat lottery play as a fun activity, not a guaranteed path to wealth. Enjoy the excitement of the draw, celebrate small wins, and prioritize fun over potential winnings.

- **Practice Responsible Budgeting:**

Set clear limits on how much you spend on lottery tickets and software, including subscriptions and in-app purchases. Stick to your budget and never gamble with money you can't afford to lose.

- **Use Software Wisely:**

If you choose to use software, do so for entertainment and personalization, not as a guaranteed path to riches. Remember, random selection and personal choices still hold value.

- **Seek Help if Needed:**

If you find yourself struggling with responsible play or exceeding your budget, don't hesitate to seek help from gambling support organizations.

Remember:

- **Responsible play is paramount.**

Prioritize your financial well-being and avoid letting software lead you to overspend.

- **Software has limitations.**

It can't predict winning numbers or guarantee success. Use it for fun, not as a strategy.

- **Focus on the experience.**

Enjoy the social aspects of the lottery, share the excitement with friends and family, and celebrate every win, big or small.

By approaching lottery software responsibly and prioritizing responsible play principles, you can ensure that your journey through this digital landscape remains enjoyable and financially sound.

Additional Tips:

- **Research software thoroughly:**

Check reviews, compare features, and understand the pricing model before purchasing.

- **Beware of hidden costs:**

Read the fine print and avoid software with hidden fees or in-app purchases that could strain your budget.

- **Don't chase losses:**

If you lose a draw, don't try to chase your losses by spending more. Stick to your budget and wait for the next draw.

- **Enjoy the social aspect:**

Play with friends or family, share the excitement of the draw, and focus on the shared experience.

Remember, responsible play is not just about software. It's about making informed choices, managing your finances wisely, and prioritizing your well-being over unrealistic expectations. Play responsibly and enjoy the journey!

Chapter 9: Understanding Lottery Syndicates and Groups: Collaboration, Communication, and Cashing In (Responsibly!)

Welcome to the exciting world of lottery syndicates and groups! This chapter will delve into the collaborative spirit of pooling resources and sharing the thrill of the lottery with friends, family, colleagues, or even online communities. But before you dive in, remember: responsible play remains our guiding star.

The Allure of Collaboration :
- **Increased Odds:**

By pooling resources, you can cover more numbers, potentially increasing your chances of winning smaller prizes, if not the jackpot itself.

- **Reduced Cost:** Sharing the cost of tickets makes participating in larger draws or buying more tickets more affordable for everyone.

- **Social Experience:**

Playing with others adds a fun and collaborative element to the lottery, turning it into a shared adventure.

- **Shared Celebration:**

Winning as a group can be even more exciting and rewarding, as you celebrate together with those who contributed.

Navigating the Maze :
- **Clear Communication:**

Establishing clear rules and openly communicating about expectations, contributions, and prize sharing is crucial to avoid disputes later.

- **Legal Considerations:**

Depending on your location, there might be specific legal requirements for forming a lottery syndicate. Research and comply with all relevant regulations.

- **Financial Responsibility:**

Set a clear budget for your syndicate participation and stick to it. Don't let it lead to overspending or financial strain.

- **Trust and Respect:**

Choose trustworthy members who understand and respect the agreed-upon rules and financial implications.

Building a Successful Syndicate:
- **Define Your Objectives:**

Establish whether you prioritize smaller wins or aiming for the big jackpot. This will influence your number selection and budget.
- **Set Clear Rules:**

Create a written agreement outlining contributions, prize distribution, dispute resolution, and communication protocols.
- **Choose Your Members Wisely:**

Select trustworthy individuals who share your financial values and commitment to responsible play.
- **Communicate Openly:**

Maintain open communication throughout, addressing concerns promptly and ensuring everyone feels heard.

Remember:
- **Responsible play is paramount.**

Prioritize your financial well-being and avoid exceeding your limits.
- **Legal compliance is crucial.**

Understand and follow all relevant regulations to avoid legal issues.
- **Clear communication and agreements are essential.**

Ensure everyone involved is on the same page to prevent future disputes.

Beyond the Basics:
This chapter will also explore:
- **Different syndicate structures:**

From informal groups to formal partnerships, we'll discuss options to suit your needs.
- **Tax implications:**

Understanding how syndicate winnings are taxed can help you plan accordingly.
- **Online platforms:**

Discover resources for finding or creating syndicates online, ensuring responsible practices are followed.

By understanding the benefits and challenges of lottery syndicates, approaching them with responsible play principles, and prioritizing clear communication, you can create a fun and rewarding experience for everyone involved. So, gather your team, establish your plan, and embark on this collaborative lottery adventure!

Remember, the true jackpot is the shared experience, the excitement of the draw, and the joy of celebrating (even small) wins together. Play responsibly, have fun, and who knows, you might just strike gold (or at least silver!) as a team.

Finding Reputable Syndicates and Managing Expectations: A Guide for Savvy Players

While lottery syndicates offer a fun and potentially cost-effective way to play, approaching them with caution and responsible play principles is crucial. Here's a comprehensive guide to finding reputable syndicates and managing expectations:

Finding Reputable Syndicates :

- **Word-of-mouth:**

Look for syndicates formed by friends, family, or colleagues you trust. This way, you have a personal connection and understanding of their financial responsibility and commitment.

- **Local organizations:**

Many community centers, sports clubs, or charity groups organize syndicates. These options offer a sense of accountability and transparency.

- **Online platforms:**

Websites and apps dedicated to lottery syndicates exist, but **proceed with caution**. Research the platform's reputation, user reviews, and legal compliance thoroughly before joining.

- **Legal requirements:**

Depending on your location, there might be regulations regarding forming and joining syndicates. Ensure the syndicate you consider adheres to all legal requirements.

Managing Expectations :
- **Understand the odds:**

Remember, even with a syndicate, winning the jackpot remains highly improbable. Focus on the fun and social aspects of playing together.

- **Set realistic budgets:**

Determine how much you're comfortable spending and stick to it. Don't let the excitement of a syndicate tempt you to overspend.

- **Clear communication:**

Discuss openly with members about expectations regarding contributions, prize distribution, and communication protocols. Establish a written agreement for clarity.

- **Celebrate small wins:**

Don't solely focus on the jackpot. Appreciate and celebrate even small wins as a group to maintain enthusiasm and responsible play.

- **Beware of unrealistic claims:**

Avoid syndicates promising guaranteed wins or claiming to "crack the code." Remember, lottery draws are random, and no method can predict the outcome.

Additional Tips:
- **Research the organizer:**

If joining an online syndicate, research the organizer's background, track record, and user reviews to assess their trustworthiness.

- **Read the fine print:**

Before joining any syndicate, carefully review the terms and conditions, including fees, payout structures, and dispute resolution procedures.

- **Seek professional advice:**

If unsure about legal or financial implications, consider consulting a lawyer or financial advisor for guidance.

Remember:
- **Responsible play is paramount.**

Prioritize your financial well-being and avoid exceeding your limits.

- **Trust and communication are key.**

Choose trustworthy members and communicate openly to avoid misunderstandings and disputes.

- **Enjoy the journey.**

Focus on the social aspects, the excitement of the draw, and celebrating wins together, regardless of their size.

By following these guidelines and approaching lottery syndicates with a responsible and discerning mindset, you can create a fun and rewarding experience for everyone involved. Remember, the true prize is the shared experience, not just the potential winnings. Play responsibly, manage expectations, and have fun on your collaborative lottery adventure!

Navigating the Legal and Tax Maze: A Guide to Responsible Group Lottery Play

While lottery syndicates and group play can be a fun and potentially cost-effective way to participate, it's crucial to navigate the legal and tax implications before diving in. Let's delve into the key considerations for responsible and informed group play:

Legal Considerations:
- **Formation and Regulations:**

Depending on your location, there might be specific legal requirements for forming a lottery syndicate. These could involve:
- **Registration:**

Some jurisdictions require syndicates to register with a regulatory body.
- **Agreements:**

Having a written agreement outlining contributions, prize distribution, and dispute resolution is essential.
- **Tax implications:**

Understanding tax obligations as a syndicate and for individual members is crucial.
- **Responsible Gambling:**

Remember, all gambling regulations, including age restrictions and responsible play principles, still apply to syndicate participation.

Tax Implications:
- **Syndicate Taxation:**

Depending on your location, winnings might be taxed differently for a syndicate compared to individual wins. Research and understand the applicable tax rules in your jurisdiction.

- **Individual Taxation:**

Each member's share of the winnings might be subject to individual income tax, depending on their tax bracket and other relevant factors.

- **Reporting Requirements:**

Syndicates might have reporting requirements to tax authorities regarding winnings and individual payouts. Consult a tax advisor for specific guidance.

Additional Tips:
- **Seek Legal Advice:**

If unsure about the legal or tax implications of forming a syndicate, consult a lawyer or tax advisor for specific guidance in your jurisdiction.

- **Clear Communication:**

Open and transparent communication among members is crucial to avoid disputes and ensure everyone understands their legal and tax obligations.

- **Record Keeping:**

Maintain accurate records of contributions, winnings, and payouts for transparency and potential tax purposes.

Remember:
- **Responsible play is paramount.**

Prioritize your financial well-being and avoid exceeding your limits.

- **Legal compliance is key.**

Understand and follow all relevant regulations to avoid legal issues.

- **Seek professional guidance when needed.**

Don't hesitate to consult legal or tax professionals to ensure responsible and informed participation.

By being aware of the legal and tax considerations, approaching group play with responsible practices, and seeking professional guidance when needed, you can ensure that your syndicate experience is fun, rewarding, and compliant with all relevant regulations.

Happy (and responsible) group play!

The Cornerstone of Collaboration: Clear Communication and Agreements in Lottery Syndicates

The allure of lottery syndicates lies in sharing the cost, increasing odds, and amplifying the excitement with friends and family. However, the foundation for a successful and harmonious syndicate rests on two crucial pillars: **clear communication** and **well-defined agreements**.

Clear Communication: The Lifeblood of Collaboration

- **Open and honest discussions:**

From the outset, openly discuss expectations, contributions, prize distribution, and communication protocols. This fosters trust and prevents misunderstandings later.

- **Regular updates:**

Keep everyone informed about ticket purchases, draws, and any relevant developments. Transparency builds trust and avoids confusion.

- **Addressing concerns promptly:**

Don't shy away from difficult conversations. Address concerns and questions openly and respectfully to maintain a positive atmosphere.

- **Preferred communication channels:**

Establish clear channels for communication, whether it's email, group chats, or regular meetings. This ensures everyone receives timely information.

Agreements: Setting the Ground Rules for Partnership

- **Written agreement:**

A written document outlining contributions, prize distribution, dispute resolution, and communication protocols protects everyone's interests and prevents future disagreements.

- **Clearly defined roles:**

Assign roles for tasks like ticket purchase, prize collection, and communication to ensure smooth operation and accountability.

- **Financial transparency:**

Clearly outline contribution amounts, ticket costs, and how winnings will be distributed based on contribution or agreed-upon percentages.

- **Dispute resolution process:**

Establish clear steps to resolve any disagreements or conflicts that might arise. This ensures fairness and prevents escalation.

- **Review and update:**

Regularly review and update the agreement to reflect changes in membership, contributions, or other relevant factors.

The Benefits of Open Communication and Agreements:

- **Reduced conflict:**

Clear communication and agreements minimize the risk of misunderstandings and disagreements, fostering a more harmonious group experience.

- **Increased trust:**

Transparency and defined expectations build trust among members, strengthening the syndicate's foundation.

- **Fairness and accountability:**

Clearly outlined rules ensure everyone contributes fairly and receives their rightful share of any winnings.

- **Long-term success:**

By establishing clear communication and agreements, you lay the groundwork for a successful and enjoyable syndicate experience in the long run.

Remember:

- **Clear communication and agreements are not one-time events.**

They are ongoing processes that require continuous effort from all members.

- **Seek professional guidance if needed.**

If unsure about legal or financial implications, consulting a lawyer or financial advisor can provide valuable insights.

By prioritizing clear communication, establishing strong agreements, and fostering a spirit of collaboration, you can turn your lottery syndicate into a fun, rewarding, and responsible adventure for everyone involved!

Chapter 10: Unveiling the Mind Game: Game Theory and Psychology in Lottery Play

We've explored the world of numbers, strategies, and collaboration. Now, let's delve into the fascinating realm of **game theory and psychology**, where the human mind plays a crucial role in the lottery experience. Remember, responsible play remains our guiding star as we explore these intriguing concepts.

Game Theory: The Logic Behind the Choices:
- **Understanding incentives:**

Game theory examines how individuals make decisions based on potential rewards and risks. Applying this to the lottery, we can analyze how players choose numbers, react to wins and losses, and interact within syndicates.

- **Nash Equilibrium:**

This concept explores finding strategies where no player has an incentive to change their decision, even if they know what others are doing. Can it be applied to lottery play?

- **Prediction vs. Influence:**

While game theory sheds light on decision-making patterns, it cannot predict individual choices due to the inherent randomness of the lottery.

Psychology: The Minds Behind the Numbers:
- **Cognitive biases:**

We all have biases that influence our choices, like the hot hand fallacy (believing past wins make future wins more likely) or the sunk cost fallacy (justifying continued play due to past investments). Understanding these biases can help us make more informed decisions.

- **Emotions and the lottery:**

The excitement of the draw, the thrill of a win, and the disappointment of a loss can trigger various emotions. Recognizing and managing these emotions is crucial for responsible play.

- **Social influences:**

Playing with friends or family can influence our choices and behaviors. It's important to communicate openly and avoid peer pressure that might lead to irresponsible play.

Responsible Play in the Mind Game:
- **Be aware of your biases:**

Recognize your own cognitive biases and how they might influence your lottery decisions.
- **Manage your emotions:**

Don't let excitement, disappointment, or frustration cloud your judgment. Stick to your budget and responsible play practices.
- **Play for entertainment, not riches:**

Don't base your financial well-being on lottery wins. Focus on the fun and social aspects of the game.
- **Seek help if needed:**

If you struggle with responsible play, don't hesitate to seek help from gambling support organizations.

Remember :
- **Game theory and psychology offer insights, not guarantees.**

They can help you understand decision-making patterns, but they cannot predict winning numbers or individual choices.

Responsible play is paramount.

Always prioritize your financial well-being and avoid letting game theory or psychology influence you into irresponsible choices.
- **The mind game is an ongoing journey.**

Continuously learn, adapt, and prioritize responsible play for a truly rewarding lottery experience.

Beyond the Basics:
This chapter will delve deeper into:
- Specific cognitive biases relevant to the lottery.
- Strategies for managing emotions and making informed decisions.
- The role of social psychology in lottery syndicates.
- The ethical considerations of using psychology in marketing and advertising related to gambling.

By understanding the insights offered by game theory and psychology, and by prioritizing responsible play principles, you can navigate the mind game of the lottery with awareness, enjoyment, and a healthy dose of skepticism. So, unlock the fascinating world of these disciplines, but always remember, responsible play is the true jackpot!

Chapter 11: Unveiling the Inner Game: Understanding the Psychology of Lottery Players

In our exploration of the lottery, we've tackled numbers, strategies, and collaboration. Now, we delve into the fascinating realm of **psychology**, where the human mind takes center stage. Remember, responsible play remains our guiding star as we uncover the thoughts, biases, and motivations behind the choices lottery players make.

Demystifying the Lottery Mindset :
- **Hope and the pursuit of dreams:**
The lottery offers a glimmer of hope for a better life, tapping into our desire for financial freedom and achieving dreams. This powerful emotion can fuel participation, but it's crucial to manage expectations and prioritize responsible play.
- **Cognitive Biases:**
We all have mental shortcuts that influence our decisions, like the **hot hand fallacy** (believing past wins increase future chances) or the **sunk cost fallacy** (justifying continued play due to past investments). Understanding these biases helps us make informed choices and avoid impulsive decisions.
- **Loss aversion and near misses:**
We tend to feel losses more intensely than wins, and near misses (almost winning) can be particularly frustrating. Recognizing these emotions and managing them is crucial for responsible play and avoiding chasing losses.
- **Social influences:**
Playing with friends or family can influence our choices and behaviors. Open communication and avoiding peer pressure are essential to maintain responsible play practices within groups.

Responsible Play in the Mind Maze:
- **Acknowledge your biases:**
Be aware of your own cognitive biases and how they might influence your lottery decisions. Don't let hope or the allure of "near misses" lead you astray.

- **Manage your emotions:** Don't let excitement, disappointment, or frustration cloud your judgment. Stick to your budget and responsible play practices.
- **Set realistic expectations:**
Remember, the odds of winning the jackpot are incredibly low. Focus on the fun and social aspects of the game, not unrealistic dreams of riches.
- **Seek help if needed:**
If you struggle with responsible play, don't hesitate to seek help from gambling support organizations.

Beyond the Basics:
This chapter will delve deeper into:
- Specific cognitive biases relevant to the lottery, like the gambler's fallacy and the availability heuristic.
- Strategies for managing emotions and making informed decisions, such as setting limits and taking breaks.
- The role of social psychology in lottery syndicates and group play.
- The ethical considerations of using psychology in marketing and advertising related to gambling.

Remember:
- **Psychological insights offer understanding, not guarantees.**
They can help you understand decision-making patterns, but they cannot predict individual choices or winning numbers.
- **Responsible play is paramount.**
Always prioritize your financial well-being and avoid letting psychological factors influence you into irresponsible choices.
- **The mind game is an ongoing journey.**
Continuously learn, adapt, and prioritize responsible play for a truly rewarding lottery experience.

By understanding the psychology of lottery players, you can navigate the mental landscape of the game with awareness, enjoyment, and a healthy dose of skepticism. So, unlock the fascinating world of psychology, but always remember, responsible play is the true jackpot!

Applying game theory to make strategic decisions

While game theory can offer valuable insights and frameworks for analyzing strategic decision-making, it's important to remember its limitations when applying it to the lottery. Here's a breakdown of its potential benefits and limitations:

Benefits of Game Theory:
- **Understanding incentives:**

By analyzing the potential rewards and risks associated with different choices, game theory can help you understand the incentives of other players (e.g., syndicate members, potential competitors for specific number combinations).
- **Identifying optimal strategies:**

In certain situations where the game has well-defined rules and perfect information (which the lottery doesn't), game theory can help identify optimal strategies based on expected outcomes.
- **Predicting group behavior:**

If you're in a syndicate, game theory can help anticipate how your fellow members might react to different decisions you make, potentially aiding in collaborative strategies.

Limitations of Game Theory:
- **Randomness:**

The lottery is inherently random, and game theory cannot predict the outcome of future draws. No strategy can guarantee a win.
- **Limited information:**

Players in the lottery rarely have complete information about other players' choices or strategies, making it difficult to apply game theory effectively.
- **Psychological factors:**

Game theory primarily focuses on rational decision-making, but human emotions and biases significantly influence lottery choices, making predictions unreliable.

Responsible Play Considerations:
- **Don't rely solely on game theory:**

Use it as a tool to understand incentives and potential outcomes, but don't base your decisions solely on its predictions.

- **Avoid unrealistic expectations:**
- Remember, the odds of winning the jackpot are extremely low. Game theory can't change that.
- **Focus on responsible play:**

Prioritize your budget and avoid exceeding your limits, regardless of what game theory might suggest.

Alternative approaches for strategic decisions:
- **Personal preferences:**

Choose numbers that hold personal significance or use random selection for an unpredictable experience.
- **Syndicate collaboration:**

Discuss and agree on strategies within your syndicate based on shared goals and budget.
- **Understanding probability:** Learn basic probability concepts to gain a general understanding of how random draws work.

Remember:
- **Game theory is a complex field with limitations.**

It's not a magic formula for winning the lottery.
- **Responsible play is paramount.**

Always prioritize your financial well-being and avoid risky decisions.
- **Enjoy the process:**

Focus on the fun and social aspects of the game, not just the potential winnings.

By understanding the potential benefits and limitations of game theory, you can make informed decisions and enjoy the lottery experience responsibly.

Maintaining a Healthy and Balanced Approach to Lottery Play: A Guide for Responsible Players

The lottery offers excitement and a chance to dream big, but it's crucial to approach it with a **healthy and balanced perspective**. Here are key principles for responsible play and maintaining a positive lottery experience:

Focus on Enjoyment, Not Riches:

- **Remember the odds:** Winning the jackpot is highly improbable. View lottery play as entertainment, not a guaranteed path to wealth.
- **Celebrate small wins:**
Celebrate even small wins to enhance the fun and avoid disappointment if you don't win big.
- **Share the experience:** Play with friends or family, or join a reputable syndicate, to share the excitement and socialize around the game.
- **Set realistic expectations:**
Don't base financial decisions or well-being on potential lottery winnings.

Practice Responsible Play :

- **Set a budget and stick to it:**
Determine how much you're comfortable spending and never exceed that limit.
- **Don't chase losses:** If you lose, don't try to recoup your losses by spending more. Stick to your budget and wait for the next draw.
- **Prioritize financial well-being:**
Ensure lottery spending doesn't impact your essential needs or financial obligations.
- **Seek help if needed:**
If you struggle with responsible play, don't hesitate to seek help from gambling support organizations.

Mindset and Decision-Making :

- **Be aware of biases:**
Understand how cognitive biases like the sunk cost fallacy or the hot hand fallacy can influence your choices. Make informed decisions based on reason, not emotions.
- **Manage your emotions:**
Don't let excitement, disappointment, or frustration cloud your judgment. Stick to your responsible play practices.
- **Avoid unrealistic promises:**
Ignore claims of guaranteed wins or strategies to "crack the code." The lottery is random, and no method can predict the outcome.

- **Focus on the present:**

Enjoy the anticipation and excitement of the draw, but don't dwell on potential winnings or dwell on losses.

Additional Tips:
- **Play for fun, not desperation:**

If you feel pressured or desperate, step away from the lottery and focus on activities that bring genuine joy.
- **Explore alternatives:**

Consider other forms of entertainment or hobbies that offer excitement and fulfillment without financial risks.
- **Educate yourself:**

Learn about responsible gambling practices and resources available to support healthy play habits.

Remember:
- **Responsible play is paramount.**

Always prioritize your financial well-being and mental health.
- **The lottery is entertainment, not a financial solution.**

Enjoy the game responsibly and within your means.
- **Focus on the journey, not just the destination.**

Appreciate the social aspects, the excitement of the draw, and celebrating wins (big or small).

By embracing these principles and prioritizing responsible play, you can ensure that your lottery experience is enjoyable, balanced, and contributes to your overall well-being. Remember, the true prize is the fun, the shared experiences, and the enjoyment of the game itself, not just the potential for big wins.

Part 4: Playing the Odds, Not Your Finances: A Guide to Responsible Lottery Play and Financial Management.

The lottery whispers sweet dreams of financial freedom, but the reality is, navigating its waters requires more than just crossing your fingers. In Part 4, we dive beyond the thrill of the draw and delve into the crucial world of **responsible play and financial management**. Forget chasing rainbows and start building a solid foundation for a truly rewarding lottery experience.

Why responsible play?

It's not about raining on your parade, but about ensuring the fun doesn't turn into a financial storm. Think of it as having a map and compass for this exciting yet potentially risky terrain. We'll equip you with the knowledge and tools to:

- **Navigate the psychology of the game:**
Understand how your brain plays tricks on you, from the allure of "hot numbers" to the trap of chasing losses. Make informed decisions, not impulsive ones fueled by excitement or disappointment.

- **Master the legal and financial landscape:**
Demystify tax implications, legal regulations, and responsible gambling practices. Play within the boundaries, safeguard your finances, and avoid any unwanted surprises.

- **Become a budgeting pro:**
Set clear spending limits, track your tickets, and make informed choices about how much you're willing to risk. Remember, responsible play is all about staying in control.

- **Manage your emotions:**
Don't let excitement cloud your judgment or disappointment lead to reckless spending. Learn to celebrate small wins and walk away when needed.

- **Play smart, play together:**
Choosing reputable vendors, understanding syndicate legalities, and maintaining clear communication within groups are key to a safe and enjoyable experience for everyone.

But responsible play isn't just about individual actions.
We'll also explore:

- **The ethical considerations of lottery advertising and marketing:** Understand how these tactics can influence your choices and how to approach them with a critical eye.
- **The impact of the lottery on communities:**
Explore the potential social and economic implications of lottery participation, both positive and negative.
- **Resources for support:**
If you or someone you know struggles with responsible play, we'll provide information on support organizations and resources available to help.

Remember, **responsible play isn't about taking the fun out of the lottery.** It's about ensuring that fun doesn't come at the expense of your financial well-being. By embracing these principles, you can transform the lottery from a fleeting thrill into a source of genuine enjoyment, shared experiences, and responsible entertainment – a win-win situation for everyone involved.

So, buckle up and join us on this journey. Let's turn the lottery from a game of chance into a game of informed choices, responsible actions, and a truly rewarding experience.

Chapter 12: Budgeting for Lottery Play: Keeping the Fun Within Your Means

The lottery's allure lies in the possibility of transforming dreams into reality, but that shouldn't come at the expense of your financial well-being. **Part 4: Playing the Odds, Not Your Finances** continues with this Chapter, where we delve into the crucial realm of **budgeting for lottery play**.

Remember, responsible play is paramount. This chapter equips you with the tools and strategies to:

Understand the Importance of Budgeting:
- **Prioritize essential needs:**
Your budget should prioritize essential expenses like housing, food, and healthcare before allocating any funds for entertainment, including the lottery.
- **Set realistic limits:**
Determine a comfortable amount you can afford to spend on the lottery without impacting your financial stability.
- **Avoid debt:** Never use credit cards, loans, or other forms of debt to finance lottery participation.

Crafting Your Lottery Budget:
- **Track your expenses:**
Monitor your overall spending habits to understand where your money goes and identify areas for potential savings.
- **Allocate a specific amount:**
Allocate a fixed amount from your entertainment budget specifically for lottery play. Stick to this limit religiously.
- **Track your lottery spending:**
Keep a record of your lottery purchases to ensure you stay within your allocated budget.

Practical Budgeting Tips:
- **Start small:**
Begin with smaller ticket purchases and gradually increase your spend only if your budget allows and responsible play principles are met.

- **Choose wisely:**

Consider the cost-effectiveness of different lottery types. For example, smaller, more frequent draws might be better for budget-conscious players.

- **Resist impulsive spending:**

Don't let excitement or chasing losses lure you into exceeding your budget. Stick to your plan and avoid impulsive purchases.

- **Celebrate small wins:**

Celebrate even small wins to enhance the fun and avoid disappointment if you don't win big. Remember, responsible play is still enjoyable!

Remember:

- **Budgeting is an ongoing process:**

Regularly review and adjust your budget as your financial situation or priorities change.

- **Seek help if needed:**

If you struggle with budgeting or responsible play, don't hesitate to seek help from financial advisors or gambling support organizations.

Beyond the Basics:

This chapter will also explore:

- **The impact of inflation on lottery budgets:**

Learn to adjust your spending based on rising costs to maintain responsible play.

- **Financial planning for potential wins:**

If you win big, understand the importance of responsible financial planning and seeking professional advice.

- **The ethical considerations of lottery advertising and budgeting:**

Be aware of how marketing tactics might influence your spending decisions.

By prioritizing responsible play, setting realistic limits, and implementing effective budgeting strategies, you ensure that the lottery remains an enjoyable form of entertainment without jeopardizing your financial well-being. Remember, a healthy budget and responsible play are the true winning tickets to a rewarding lottery experience.

Chapter 13: Mastering the Limits: Setting and Sticking to Responsible Lottery Spending

The thrill of chasing a dream comes with a responsibility: **financial prudence**. In Part 4 of our guide, we delve into **Chapter 10: Setting Realistic Spending Limits and Sticking to Them**, equipping you with the tools to navigate the lottery responsibly and within your means.

Remember, responsible play is the cornerstone of a truly rewarding lottery experience. This chapter empowers you to:

Craft Realistic Spending Limits:
- **Prioritize Needs over Entertainment:**

Essential expenses like food, housing, and healthcare come first. Allocate lottery funds only after fulfilling these crucial needs.

- **Know Your Financial Reality:**

Honestly assess your income and expenses to determine a comfortable amount you can dedicate to lottery play without impacting your financial stability.

- **Start Small and Grow Gradually:**

Begin with smaller limits and gradually increase only if your budget allows and responsible play principles are upheld.

Sticking to Your Limits:
- **Create a Budget and Track Expenses:**

Develop a comprehensive budget, allocating a specific amount for lottery play within your entertainment category. Track your spending meticulously to stay within your limit.

- **Resist Impulsive Purchases:**

Avoid the lure of excitement or chasing losses. Remember, your budget is your safeguard against impulsive decisions.

- **Choose Cost-Effective Options:**

Consider smaller, more frequent draws or less expensive ticket options to make your budget stretch further.

- **Celebrate Small Wins:**

Appreciating even minor wins enhances the fun and prevents disappointment if a big win eludes you.

Beyond the Basics:
- **Adjust for Inflation:**

Regularly review your budget and adjust your spending limits to account for rising costs, ensuring responsible play even amidst economic changes.

- **Plan for Potential Wins:** If you win big, seek professional financial advice to manage your windfall responsibly and avoid impulsive spending.

- **Be Aware of Marketing Tactics:**

Understand how lottery advertising might influence your spending decisions and remain critical of unrealistic portrayals of wins.

Remember:
- **Setting limits is just the first step.**

Sticking to them requires commitment and discipline.

- **Seek Help if Needed:**

Don't hesitate to reach out to financial advisors or gambling support organizations if you struggle with budgeting or responsible play.

Beyond Individual Limits:

This chapter will also explore:

- **Setting limits within syndicates:**

Establish clear spending agreements and communication channels within group play to ensure everyone adheres to responsible limits.

- **The legal and ethical considerations of spending limits:**

Understand how regulations and responsible gambling practices shape legal limits on lottery spending.

By setting realistic spending limits, prioritizing financial well-being, and employing effective strategies to stick to your plan, you transform the lottery from a gamble into a fun and controlled form of entertainment. Remember, responsible play is the true winning ticket to a truly rewarding lottery experience.

Chapter 14: Balancing Dreams and Reality: Prioritizing Financial Obligations and Goals in Lottery Play

In Part 4 of our guide, we continue our journey into **responsible play and financial management**. In Chapter 11, we tackle the crucial concept of **prioritizing financial obligations and goals** before engaging in any form of lottery play, including the exciting, yet potentially risky, world of lottery tickets.

Remember, responsible play is not about suppressing fun, but about approaching the lottery with awareness and respect for your financial well-being. This chapter empowers you to:

Understand the Importance of Prioritization:

- **Needs vs. Wants:**

Clearly differentiate between essential needs like housing, food, and healthcare from discretionary wants like entertainment, including the lottery.

- **Financial Goals:**

Identify your short- and long-term financial goals, such as saving for a down payment, retirement, or education. These goals should take precedence over lottery spending.

- **Debt Management:**

If you have outstanding debt, prioritize paying it off before allocating any funds to lottery play. Remember, debt can quickly spiral out of control and impact your financial stability.

Making Informed Choices:

- **Budgeting for Needs and Goals:**

Allocate your income first to cover essential needs and then towards achieving your financial goals through savings and responsible investments.

- **Lottery as Entertainment:**

View lottery participation as a form of entertainment, not a path to financial freedom. Allocate only a small portion of your entertainment budget to lottery play.

- **Cost vs. Potential Reward:**

Weigh the cost of lottery tickets against the highly improbable chance of winning big. Remember, the odds are heavily stacked against you.

Strategies for Responsible Play:
- **Set Spending Limits:**

Establish a fixed amount you can afford to spend on the lottery without impacting your ability to meet needs and achieve financial goals. Stick to this limit religiously.

- **Track Your Spending:**

Monitor your lottery expenses alongside your overall spending to ensure you stay within your budget and financial priorities.

- **Avoid Chasing Losses:** If you lose, don't try to recoup your losses by spending more. Stick to your budget and wait for the next draw.

- **Celebrate Small Wins:**

Appreciate even small wins to enhance the fun and avoid disappointment if a big win eludes you.

Remember:
- **Prioritization is an ongoing process:**

Regularly review your financial situation, goals, and spending habits to ensure responsible play remains at the forefront.

- **Seek Help if Needed:**

If you struggle with prioritizing financial obligations or responsible play, don't hesitate to seek help from financial advisors or gambling support organizations.

Beyond Individual Choices:

This chapter will also explore:

- **The impact of lottery advertising on financial priorities:** Understand how marketing tactics might influence your spending decisions and prioritize your financial well-being.

The social and economic implications of lottery play: Be aware of the potential impact of lottery participation on communities and individuals, considering both positive and negative aspects.

- **Resources for financial literacy and responsible gambling:**

Learn about tools and support available to make informed financial decisions and prioritize your well-being.

By prioritizing financial obligations and goals, making informed choices, and implementing effective strategies for responsible play, you ensure that the lottery remains an enjoyable form of entertainment without jeopardizing your financial future. Remember, responsible play is the true winning ticket to a truly rewarding lottery experience.

Chapter 15: Outsmarting Impulses: Defeating the Urge to Overspend on the Lottery

The lottery's allure lies in the instant thrill of chasing big dreams. But within this excitement lurks a hidden danger: **impulsive spending and debt**. In Chapter 12 of Part 4: Responsible Play and Financial Management, we equip you with the tools to **outmaneuver impulsive urges and safeguard your financial well-being**.

Remember, responsible play is the cornerstone of a rewarding lottery experience. This chapter empowers you to:

Understand the Psychology of Impulsive Purchases:
- **Emotional Triggers:**

Identify the emotions, like boredom, excitement, or frustration, that can fuel impulsive lottery purchases.
- **Cognitive Biases:**

Recognize how cognitive biases like the "hot hand fallacy" or the sunk cost fallacy can influence your decisions, leading to irrational spending.
- **Marketing Tactics:**

Be aware of how lottery advertising and marketing exploit your emotions and biases, encouraging impulsive choices.

Defeating Impulsive Urges:
- **Set Spending Limits:**

Establish a fixed budget for lottery play, ensuring it doesn't jeopardize essential expenses or debt repayment.
- **Implement Cooling Off Periods:**

Before buying a ticket, wait for at least 24 hours to allow the initial excitement to fade and make a rational decision.
- **Avoid Playing When Emotional:**

Don't play when feeling stressed, depressed, or overly excited, as these emotions can cloud your judgment.
- **Use Cash:** Opt for cash instead of credit cards to limit your spending and avoid accumulating debt.

Managing Debt and Responsible Play:
- **Prioritize Debt Repayment:**

If you have outstanding debt, prioritize paying it off before allocating any funds to the lottery. Remember, debt can quickly spiral out of control and hinder your financial goals.

- **Seek Help if Needed:**

Don't hesitate to reach out to debt counselors or financial advisors if you struggle with managing debt or responsible play.

Beyond the Basics:
- **The impact of social pressure:**

Understand how peer pressure or group dynamics within syndicates can influence impulsive spending.

- **The legal and ethical considerations of impulse purchases:**

Be aware of regulations and responsible gambling practices that aim to protect consumers from impulsive spending on lotteries.

- **Resources for responsible gambling and debt management:**

Learn about tools and support available to help you make informed financial decisions and avoid impulsive spending.

By understanding the psychology of impulsive purchases, implementing strategies to resist them, and prioritizing debt repayment, you transform the lottery from a potential financial pitfall into a controlled form of entertainment. Remember, responsible play is the true winning ticket to a truly rewarding lottery experience.

Bonus Tip: Consider setting up automatic transfers to savings or debt repayment accounts, making it harder to access funds for impulsive lottery purchases.

Remember, you have the power to make informed choices and prioritize your financial well-being. Play smart, play responsibly, and enjoy the lottery for what it is: entertainment, not a guaranteed path to riches.

Chapter 16: Financial Planning for Lottery Winnings

Imagine the elation of matching the winning numbers, the champagne showers, and the dreams of a life transformed. But amidst the initial euphoria, a crucial question arises: how do you translate that windfall into lasting security and fulfillment? This chapter delves into the critical realm of financial planning for lottery winnings, guiding you through the complex decisions that come with sudden wealth.

Beyond the Glitter: Seeking Professional Guidance

Winning the lottery thrusts you into uncharted financial territory. While the allure of splurging and living the high life may be tempting, navigating such a complex landscape requires expert advice. This chapter emphasizes the importance of seeking professional financial advisors, experienced navigators who can chart a course for your newfound fortune. They can:

Craft a personalized plan: Tailored to your unique goals, risk tolerance, and financial situation.

Decode tax implications: Ensure you understand and comply with complex tax obligations associated with lottery winnings.

Navigate investment strategies: Guide you towards diversified portfolios that maximize your wealth and mitigate risk.

Protect your assets: Help you avoid scams and safeguard your windfall from potential predators.

From Windfall to Legacy: Managing Wisely and Avoiding Scams

Suddenly holding a significant sum can cloud your judgment. This chapter empowers you to manage your winnings wisely, avoiding impulsive decisions and predatory schemes. Here are some key strategies:

Resist the urge to splurge: Develop a spending plan that prioritizes essential needs and long-term goals over instant gratification.

Beware of "get-rich-quick" schemes: Scammers often target lottery winners. This chapter equips you with red flags to identify and avoid fraudulent investment opportunities.

Pay off high-interest debt: Prioritize eliminating costly debt before investing or making significant purchases.

Consider establishing a trust: This legal framework protects your assets and ensures responsible management of your wealth.

Building a Secure Future: Investing for Long-Term Security

Winning the lottery is a rare opportunity to secure your future, but it's not a free pass to endless luxury. This chapter emphasizes the importance of investing your winnings wisely for long-term security. Here's how:

Diversify your portfolio: Spread your investments across various asset classes, such as stocks, bonds, and real estate, to mitigate risk.

Invest for the long term: Don't chase short-term gains. Focus on building a sustainable financial foundation for yourself and future generations.

Consider your risk tolerance: Work with your financial advisor to determine the investment strategies that align with your comfort level with risk.

Reinvest earnings: Don't just spend the income from your investments. Reinvesting it allows your wealth to compound and grow over time.

Remember: Winning the lottery is not just about the money; it's about making informed choices to secure your future and create a life filled with purpose and meaning. By seeking professional guidance, managing your windfall wisely, and investing strategically, you can transform your lottery win into a steppingstone to a fulfilling and prosperous future.

This introduction sets the stage for a comprehensive exploration of financial planning for lottery winners, highlighting the key steps and strategies for navigating this important yet complex aspect of sudden wealth.

Seeking professional financial advice

While I can't offer specific financial advice myself, I can definitely help you understand the importance of seeking professional help and guide you towards resources that can assist you. Here are some key points to consider:

Why Seek Professional Advice?

Complexity of financial planning: Managing a large windfall involves various decisions, including taxes, investments, estate planning, and more. Professionals can navigate these complexities and create a personalized plan for your unique situation.

Emotional impact: Winning big can be emotionally overwhelming, and professionals can help you manage these emotions and make informed decisions without letting them cloud your judgment.

Avoiding mistakes: Inexperience with large sums of money can lead to costly mistakes. Professionals can guide you towards sound financial strategies and help you avoid common pitfalls.

What to Look for in a Financial Advisor:

Credentials and experience: Choose an advisor with relevant certifications and experience in managing windfalls and wealth management.

Fiduciary duty: Ensure they operate under a fiduciary duty, legally obligated to act in your best interests.

Transparency and communication: Choose someone who clearly communicates their fees, investment strategies, and potential risks involved.

Additional Resources:

The National Endowment for Financial Education (NEFE): https://www.nefe.org/

The Financial Planning Association (FPA): https://www.plannersearch.org/

The National Association of Personal Financial Advisors (NAPFA): https://www.napfa.org/find-an-advisor

Remember, seeking professional financial advice is crucial even if you haven't won the lottery yet. It can help you develop a solid financial plan, manage your investments, and achieve your long-term financial goals.

Do you have any other questions about financial planning or would you like me to elaborate on any of the points mentioned above?

Managing windfalls wisely and avoiding scams

Managing a windfall, whether from a lottery win, inheritance, or other sources, requires careful planning and responsible decision-making. Here are some key points to remember:

Managing Wisely :

- **Seek professional financial advice:**

As mentioned earlier, consulting a qualified financial advisor is crucial. They can help you create a personalized plan for managing your windfall, considering taxes, investments, debt reduction, and long-term goals.

Set financial goals: Define your short- and long-term financial aspirations. Do you want to pay off debt, invest for retirement, or start a business? Having clear goals helps guide your decisions.

- **Diversify your investments:**

Don't put all your eggs in one basket. Spread your investments across various asset classes like stocks, bonds, real estate, and cash equivalents to mitigate risk.

- **Avoid impulsive spending:**

Resist the urge to splurge on luxuries. Create a budget and stick to it, prioritizing essential expenses and long-term needs over fleeting desires.

- **Beware of scams:**

Unfortunately, scammers often target individuals with windfalls. Be cautious of unsolicited investment offers, charities, or "get rich quick" schemes. Do your research and seek professional advice before making any significant financial commitments.

Avoiding Scams:

- **Do your research:**

Before investing or donating, thoroughly research the organization or individual involved. Check their credentials, reputation, and online reviews.

- **Never feel pressured:**

Legitimate opportunities won't pressure you into quick decisions. If you feel pressured, walk away.

- **Beware of unrealistic promises:**

Guarantees of high returns or quick riches are red flags. If it sounds too good to be true, it probably is.

- **Consult with a financial advisor:**

Discuss potential investments and charitable donations with your trusted advisor before committing any funds.

- **Report suspicious activity:**

If you suspect a scam, report it to the authorities and relevant organizations like the Federal Trade Commission (FTC).

Additional Resources:
- The National Endowment for Financial Education (NEFE): https://www.nefe.org/
- The Financial Planning Association (FPA): https://www.plannersearch.org/
- The Federal Trade Commission (FTC): https://www.consumer.ftc.gov/
- The Securities and Exchange Commission (SEC): https://www.sec.gov/

By seeking professional guidance, making informed decisions, and staying vigilant against scams, you can ensure that your windfall becomes a source of lasting financial security and fulfillment. Remember, responsible management is key to turning a lucky break into a stepping stone toward a brighter financial future.

Investing winnings for long-term security

Investing a lottery windfall wisely is crucial to ensuring long-term security and achieving your financial goals. Here's some guidance to help you navigate this process responsibly:

Seek Professional Help:
- **Financial advisor:**

Working with a qualified financial advisor specializing in wealth management is essential. They can assess your risk tolerance, financial goals, and develop a personalized investment strategy tailored to your unique circumstances.

- **Tax advisor:**

Understanding the tax implications of your winnings is crucial. Consulting a tax advisor helps ensure you navigate tax complexities and minimize tax liabilities.

Investing Strategies:
- **Diversification:**

Spread your investments across various asset classes like stocks, bonds, real estate, and cash equivalents to mitigate risk and achieve a balanced portfolio.

- **Long-term approach:**

Invest for the long term (5+ years) and avoid chasing short-term gains. Market fluctuations are inevitable, so focus on consistent growth over time.

- **Asset allocation:**

Your age, risk tolerance, and financial goals determine your asset allocation. Younger individuals can handle more risk and invest in growth-oriented assets like stocks, while older individuals might prioritize stability with bonds and real estate.

- **Consider professional investment management:**

Exploring options like mutual funds or robo-advisors can be beneficial if you prefer a hands-off approach or lack investment expertise.

Additional Tips:
- **Avoid emotional decisions:**

Don't let excitement or fear guide your investment choices. Stick to your long-term plan and consult your advisor before making significant changes.

- **Beware of get-rich-quick schemes:**

Legitimate investments rarely offer unrealistic returns. Research opportunities thoroughly and avoid anything promising guaranteed high profits.

- **Invest gradually:**

Don't invest your entire windfall at once. Consider dollar-cost averaging to spread out your investments over time and mitigate risk.

- **Live below your means:**

Don't inflate your lifestyle based on a sudden windfall. Continue living responsibly and avoid excessive spending.

- **Plan for future expenses:**

Factor in future expenses like education, retirement, and healthcare when making investment decisions.

Remember, responsible investing is a marathon, not a sprint. By seeking professional guidance, diversifying your portfolio, and adopting a long-term perspective, you can turn your winnings into a secure foundation for a prosperous future.

Additional Resources:
- The National Endowment for Financial Education (NEFE): https://www.nefe.org/
- The Financial Planning Association (FPA): https://www.plannersearch.org/
- The Securities and Exchange Commission (SEC): https://www.sec.gov/

By following these principles and seeking professional help, you can confidently invest your winnings and build a stable financial future for yourself and your loved ones.

Chapter 17: The Reality of Winning the Lottery: Beyond the Dream, Navigating the Change

Winning the lottery evokes images of champagne showers and dream-filled futures. But while the potential for financial freedom is undeniable, the reality of winning the lottery extends far beyond the initial euphoria. Chapter 17 dives deep into this often-overlooked aspect, equipping you with crucial knowledge and guidance to navigate the significant changes a win can bring.

Managing Expectations: Odds and the "Winner's Curse"
- ### Understanding the True Odds:
This chapter emphasizes the reality that winning the lottery is incredibly improbable. Accepting the low odds helps manage expectations and prevents disappointment.
- ### The "Winner's Curse":
Be aware of the psychological phenomenon where winners overvalue their prize, potentially leading to poor financial decisions.

Impact on Relationships and Lifestyle:
- ### Shifting Dynamics:
Winning can create tension and strain within families and friendships. Open communication and setting boundaries are crucial to maintaining healthy relationships.
- ### Lifestyle Adjustments:
Sudden wealth can lead to impulsive spending, career changes, and relocation. It's essential to make informed decisions considering your values and long-term goals.

Responsible Wealth Management:
- ### Seeking Professional Help:
Don't go it alone! Chapter 17 emphasizes the importance of seeking guidance from qualified financial advisors and tax professionals to navigate complex financial decisions.
- ### Avoiding Scams:
Unfortunately, scammers often target lottery winners. Be cautious of unsolicited investment offers and prioritize reputable advisors with your best interests at heart.

- **Long-Term Planning:**

Winning is not an excuse to abandon responsible financial practices. Chapter 17 stresses the importance of budgeting, investing wisely, and planning for the future.

Remember, winning the lottery is a life-altering event, not a fairy tale ending. This chapter equips you with the knowledge and tools to navigate the challenges and opportunities that come with sudden wealth. By managing expectations, prioritizing relationships, and seeking professional guidance, you can transform your win into a foundation for a fulfilling and secure future.

Bonus Tip: Consider establishing a trust to manage your winnings responsibly and protect your assets for yourself and your loved ones.

Remember, responsible play and informed decision-making are the true winning tickets, even beyond the jackpot.

Demystifying the Dream: Understanding Odds and Managing Expectations in the Lottery

Winning the lottery: a dream for many, a reality for few. While the allure of instant wealth is undeniable, navigating the reality of such a life-altering event requires a grounded understanding of the **odds and responsible management of expectations**. Chapter 17 of "Six Numbers to Freedom" serves as your guide to understanding the true landscape of lottery wins, empowering you to approach the game with informed optimism.

Beyond the Jackpot Hype:

- **Facing the True Odds:**

The chapter dispels the myth of guaranteed riches. It emphasizes the crucial fact that winning the lottery is incredibly improbable, highlighting the vast statistical gap between fantasy and reality. Accepting these low odds is the first step towards managing expectations and avoiding disappointment.

- **The "Winner's Curse":**

Be aware of this psychological phenomenon where winners often overvalue their prize, leading to impulsive spending and poor financial decisions. The chapter equips you with knowledge to avoid this pitfall and make informed choices.

Beyond the Initial Thrill:
- **Shifting Expectations:**

Winning isn't just about financial freedom; it can significantly impact your life. The chapter explores the potential changes in relationships, career paths, and lifestyle choices that accompany sudden wealth. It emphasizes the importance of setting realistic expectations and navigating these changes with awareness and responsibility.

- **Managing Excitement:**

Winning can trigger a surge of emotions. The chapter encourages responsible management of these emotions to prevent impulsive decisions and prioritize long-term well-being over fleeting excitement.

Building a Foundation for Success:
- **Seeking Professional Guidance:**

Don't go it alone! Chapter 17 highlights the importance of seeking guidance from qualified financial advisors and tax professionals. Their expertise can help you navigate complex financial decisions and maximize your winnings responsibly.

- **Planning for the Future:**

Winning shouldn't be an excuse to abandon responsible financial practices. The chapter emphasizes the importance of budgeting, investing wisely, and planning for the future to ensure long-term financial security.

- **Protecting Your Assets:**

Scammers often target lottery winners. The chapter equips you with awareness of potential scams and emphasizes prioritizing reputable advisors with your best interests at heart.

Remember: Winning the lottery is a rare opportunity, not a guaranteed path to a perfect life. By understanding the odds, managing expectations responsibly, and seeking professional guidance, you can transform your win into a foundation for a fulfilling and secure future.

Bonus Tip: Consider establishing a trust to manage your winnings responsibly and protect your assets for yourself and your loved ones.

Remember, responsible play and informed decision-making are the true winning tickets, even beyond the jackpot.

By understanding the true nature of lottery wins and prioritizing responsible choices, you can approach the game with informed optimism and navigate any potential windfall with clarity and foresight.

Beyond Riches: Navigating the Impact of Winning on Relationships and Lifestyle

Winning the lottery: a moment of elation, a promise of a changed life. But amidst the champagne showers and dreams of mansions, Chapter 17 of "Six Numbers to Freedom" delves into a crucial aspect often overlooked - the **impact of winning on relationships and lifestyle**. It equips you with the knowledge and tools to navigate these potential challenges and emerge with stronger connections and a fulfilling new life.

Shifting Dynamics:
- **Family and Friends:**

Sudden wealth can create tension and strain within families and friendships. Jealousy, resentment, and unsolicited advice can arise. The chapter emphasizes open communication, setting boundaries, and prioritizing genuine connections over material expectations.

- **Romantic Relationships:**

Winning can alter dynamics within romantic partnerships. The chapter explores potential issues like power imbalances, changes in lifestyle priorities, and the emergence of hidden agendas. It encourages honest communication and shared decision-making to strengthen the foundation of your relationship.

Lifestyle Adjustments:
- **Impulsive Spending:**

The temptation to splurge on luxuries is high. The chapter emphasizes the importance of creating a budget, resisting impulsive purchases, and focusing on long-term goals to avoid financial strain and regret.

- **Career Changes:**

Leaving a job, starting a business, or pursuing passions can be tempting. The chapter encourages careful consideration of your skills, interests, and financial security before making career decisions based solely on wealth.

- **Relocation:**

Moving to a new location can be exciting, but it also comes with challenges. The chapter emphasizes researching thoroughly, considering the impact on family and friends, and ensuring the move aligns with your overall goals and values.

Maintaining Balance :

- **Gratitude and Humility:**

Remember the source of your good fortune and appreciate the opportunities it brings. The chapter encourages maintaining humility and avoiding arrogance that can damage relationships.

- **Stay True to Yourself:**

Don't let wealth change your core values and personality. The chapter emphasizes staying grounded, connected to loved ones, and pursuing activities that bring you genuine joy.

- **Seek Professional Help:**

Navigating these significant life changes can be challenging. The chapter encourages seeking guidance from therapists, financial advisors, and life coaches to ensure you make informed decisions and maintain emotional well-being.

Remember: Winning the lottery is a life-altering event, not a magic solution to all life's challenges. By understanding the potential impact on relationships and lifestyle, prioritizing responsible choices, and seeking professional support, you can navigate these changes with grace, maintain healthy connections, and create a fulfilling new reality that goes beyond the initial excitement of the win.

Bonus Tip: Consider establishing a family foundation or trust to share your wealth responsibly and connect with causes you care about, strengthening your sense of purpose and community.

Remember, true wealth lies not just in material possessions, but in strong relationships, a fulfilling life, and responsible choices that ensure a brighter future for yourself and those you cherish.

Beyond the Jackpot: The Importance of Responsible Wealth Management

Winning the lottery can be like waking up with a genie at your side, whispering promises of endless possibilities. But amidst the initial euphoria, Chapter 17 of "Six Numbers to Freedom" reminds us that true success lies not just in the size of the win, but in **responsible wealth management**. This chapter serves as your compass, guiding you towards navigating sudden wealth with wisdom and foresight.

Safeguarding Your Windfall:
Seek Professional Guidance:
Don't go it alone! The chapter emphasizes the crucial role of qualified financial advisors and tax professionals. Their expertise can help you navigate complex financial decisions, avoid pitfalls, and maximize your winnings responsibly.

- **Beware of Scammers:**
Unfortunately, scammers often target lottery winners. The chapter equips you with awareness of potential scams and emphasizes prioritizing reputable advisors who have your best interests at heart.

- **Protect Your Assets:**
Consider establishing a trust to manage your winnings responsibly and protect your assets for yourself and your loved ones.

Building a Secure Future:

- **Budgeting and Planning:**
Winning shouldn't be an excuse to abandon responsible financial practices. The chapter emphasizes the importance of creating a budget, allocating funds wisely, and planning for the future to ensure long-term financial security.

- **Investing Wisely:**
Don't rush into impulsive investments. The chapter encourages diversifying your portfolio, considering your risk tolerance, and seeking professional guidance to build a sustainable investment strategy.

- **Debt Management:**
If you have outstanding debt, prioritize paying it off before splurging on luxuries. The chapter emphasizes the importance of financial responsibility and avoiding the burden of debt.

Making Informed Choices:
- **Understanding Taxes:**

Winning comes with significant tax implications. The chapter encourages consulting tax professionals to understand your tax obligations and ensure compliance.
- **Philanthropy and Giving Back:**

Consider using your wealth to support causes you care about. The chapter suggests responsible charitable giving through reputable organizations to create a positive impact beyond personal gain.
- **Long-Term Goals:**

Don't let the initial excitement cloud your vision. The chapter emphasizes defining your long-term goals and ensuring your financial decisions align with them, leading to a fulfilling and meaningful future.

Remember: Winning the lottery is a rare opportunity, not a guarantee of happiness. By prioritizing responsible wealth management, seeking professional guidance, and making informed choices, you can transform your win into a foundation for a secure, fulfilling, and impactful life.

Bonus Tip: Share your winnings responsibly with family and friends, but establish clear boundaries to avoid resentment and maintain healthy relationships.

Remember, responsible play and informed decision-making are the true winning tickets, even beyond the jackpot.

By understanding the importance of responsible wealth management and prioritizing responsible choices, you can ensure that your lottery win becomes a source of lasting joy, stability, and positive change for yourself and those around you.

Chapter 18: Beyond the Jackpot: The Enjoyment of the Game

Winning the lottery, like striking gold, is a dream for many, but an elusive reality for most. While the allure of instant wealth and a life transformed is undeniable, Chapter 18 of "Six Numbers to Freedom" shifts the focus from the jackpot to a core aspect often overlooked: **the enjoyment of the game itself**. It reminds us that true fulfillment can lie not just in the outcome, but in the journey and the mindful participation in the lottery experience.

Beyond the Dream of Riches:
- **Embracing the Fun:**

The chapter encourages approaching the lottery as a form of entertainment, a chance to indulge in a bit of harmless fun and anticipation. It emphasizes the joy of picking numbers, dreaming of possibilities, and sharing the experience with friends and family.

- **Managing Expectations:**

Winning big is statistically improbable. The chapter highlights the importance of setting realistic expectations and focusing on the enjoyment of the game itself, rather than solely fixating on the potential windfall.

Finding Joy in the Process:
- **Social Interaction:**

The chapter encourages using lottery participation as an opportunity to connect with friends, family, and even strangers through shared dreams and friendly competition.

- **Mindful Participation:**

It promotes mindful selection of numbers, analyzing past results, and strategizing with friends, turning the act of playing into a mentally stimulating and engaging activity.

- **Supporting Local Businesses:**

Remember that lottery ticket purchases often contribute to local businesses and communities. The chapter encourages acknowledging this positive impact and finding joy in supporting local establishments.

Beyond the Win or Lose:

- **Appreciating the Small Wins:**

Celebrate small wins, even minor prizes, as they add to the excitement and remind you of the inherent fun in the game.

- **Maintaining Balance:**

Don't allow the lottery to consume your life or finances. The chapter emphasizes maintaining a healthy balance, prioritizing responsibilities, and enjoying other activities and hobbies.

- **Gratitude and Contentment:**

Remember, true happiness comes not just from material possessions, but from gratitude for what you have and a fulfilling life filled with meaningful experiences.

Remember: Winning the lottery is a rare and fortunate event, but it's not the only path to happiness. By approaching the lottery as a form of entertainment, managing expectations, and finding joy in the process, you can transform the experience into a positive and enriching addition to your life, regardless of the outcome.

Bonus Tip: Use the lottery as an opportunity to explore your creativity by writing stories or poems based on your chosen numbers and potential wins.

Remember, true wealth lies not just in material possessions, but in finding joy in simple pleasures, fostering meaningful connections, and living a life filled with purpose and gratitude.

This concludes Chapter 18 of "Six Numbers to Freedom." I hope it provides a balanced and insightful approach to the lottery, reminding you that true fulfillment can be found in the journey itself, win or lose.

Chapter 19: Play Smart, Play Fun: Approaching the Lottery as Entertainment, Not a Get-Rich-Quick Scheme

"Six Numbers to Freedom" equips you with the knowledge and strategies to navigate the world of lotteries, but its ultimate message goes beyond just winning. Chapter 19 emphasizes a crucial point: **approach the lottery as entertainment, not a get-rich-quick scheme.** This shift in perspective fosters responsible play, protects your financial well-being, and allows you to enjoy the journey, regardless of the outcome.

Breaking the Myth:
- **Odds Reality Check:**

Winning the lottery is statistically improbable. The chapter reinforces the importance of understanding the true odds and managing expectations accordingly. Remember, it's a game of chance, not a guaranteed path to riches.

- **Responsible Spending:**

Allocate only a small portion of your disposable income to lottery participation. The chapter encourages budgeting and setting clear limits to avoid financial strain and prioritize essential needs.

The Fun Factor:
- **Engage in the Process:**

Embrace the thrill of picking numbers, strategizing with friends, and anticipating the draws. The chapter highlights the enjoyment of the game itself, fostering a sense of community and shared excitement.

- **Social Interaction:**

Use the lottery as a social activity. The chapter promotes playing with friends, family, or colleagues, building connections and shared experiences that go beyond the game itself.

- **Mindful Participation:**

Turn number selection into a stimulating activity. The chapter suggests analyzing past results, exploring different strategies, and engaging in friendly competition, adding a layer of intellectual challenge to the fun.

Beyond the Win or Lose:
- **Celebrate Small Victories:**

Appreciate small wins, even minor prizes. The chapter encourages recognizing and celebrating these successes, reminding you that the game offers more than just the jackpot.
- **Maintain Balance:**

The lottery is entertainment, not an obsession. The chapter emphasizes maintaining a healthy balance, prioritizing responsibilities, and pursuing other interests and hobbies that bring you fulfillment.
- **Gratitude and Contentment:**

Remember, true happiness comes from living a meaningful life filled with experiences and connections, not solely from material possessions. The chapter encourages cultivating gratitude for what you have and finding joy in the present moment.

Remember: The lottery is a game, and like any game, it should be played responsibly and enjoyed for the entertainment it provides. By managing expectations, prioritizing financial well-being, and focusing on the fun aspects, you can transform your lottery experience into a positive and enriching activity, win or lose.

Bonus Tip: Organize themed lottery gatherings with friends and family, incorporating snacks, music, and discussions around potential winnings, creating a memorable and enjoyable experience regardless of the outcome.

Remember, true wealth lies not just in material possessions, but in responsible choices, meaningful connections, and a fulfilling life filled with experiences and gratitude.

This concludes Chapter 19 of "Six Numbers to Freedom." I hope it encourages you to approach the lottery with a healthy perspective, prioritizing responsible play and enjoying the journey, regardless of the final numbers drawn.

Chapter 20: Finding Joy and Responsibility: Making the Game More Than a Dream

As "Six Numbers to Freedom" reaches its final chapter, it shifts the focus from simply understanding the lottery to finding **joy in the process and participating responsibly**. This concluding chapter emphasizes that true fulfillment comes not just from potential winnings, but from embracing the experience itself and making informed choices that ensure a secure and fulfilling life.

Cultivating Joyful Participation:
- **The Thrill of the Chase:**

Celebrate the anticipation and excitement that come with selecting numbers, dreaming big, and sharing this experience with loved ones. Remember, the journey itself can be a source of joy and connection.

- **Mindful Engagement:**

Turn number selection into a mentally stimulating activity. Explore mathematical strategies, analyze past results, and discuss possibilities with friends, adding a layer of intellectual engagement to the fun.

- **Community and Social Interaction:**

Use the lottery as a social catalyst. Organize gatherings with friends and family, share stories, and enjoy the camaraderie, regardless of the outcome. Focus on the shared experience, not just the win.

- **Small Victories Matter:**

Celebrate even minor wins, whether it's matching a few numbers or winning a free ticket. Appreciate these moments and recognize the small joys the game offers beyond the jackpot.

Playing Responsibly, Winning Wisely:
- **Prioritize Financial Well-being:**

Remember, the lottery is entertainment, not a financial safety net. Only allocate a small portion of your disposable income to playing, ensuring essential needs and financial goals are prioritized.

- **Manage Expectations:**

Understand the true odds of winning and avoid chasing quick riches. Embrace the game for its entertainment value and avoid fixating on unrealistic dreams that could lead to financial strain.

- **Seek Professional Guidance:**

If you win big, don't go it alone. Seek professional financial advice to manage your windfall responsibly, minimize taxes, and invest wisely for a secure future.

- **Philanthropy and Giving Back:**

Consider using your winnings to support causes you care about. Responsible charitable giving can create a positive impact beyond personal gain and bring greater fulfillment.

Beyond the Jackpot: True Wealth:

- **Gratitude and Contentment:**

True happiness comes from appreciating what you have, cultivating meaningful relationships, and living a fulfilling life. Don't define your worth or happiness solely by the lottery.

- **Balance and Responsible Choices:**

Maintain a healthy balance between playing the lottery and other activities and responsibilities. Prioritize your well-being, pursue your passions, and make informed choices that contribute to a thriving life.

- **Memories and Experiences:**

Remember, the most valuable treasures are not material possessions, but the memories, experiences, and connections you create along the way.

Remember: The lottery is a game, and like any game, it should be played responsibly and enjoyed for the entertainment it provides. By prioritizing responsible play, finding joy in the process, and cultivating gratitude for what you have, you can transform your lottery experience into a positive and enriching part of your life, regardless of the outcome.

Bonus Tip: Use the lottery as an opportunity to explore your creativity. Write stories or poems inspired by your chosen numbers and potential wins, adding a personal and imaginative dimension to the experience.

Remember, true wealth lies not just in material possessions, but in responsible choices, meaningful connections, and a fulfilling life filled with experiences, gratitude, and joy.

This concludes "Six Numbers to Freedom." May this message guide you to approach the lottery with a balanced perspective, find joy in the journey, and make decisions that contribute to a secure and fulfilling life, win or lose.

Part 5: Conclusion

Six Numbers to Freedom: A Roadmap to Navigating the American Lottery (Summary)

"Six Numbers to Freedom" delves into the world of American lotteries, equipping you with the knowledge and strategies to navigate this complex and potentially rewarding landscape.

Part 1: Understanding the Game:
- **Demystifying the System:**

Explore different lottery games, their rules, odds, and tax implications. Learn how to choose between matching and drawing games, state and multi-state lotteries, while considering your budget and risk tolerance.

Responsible Play: This crucial section emphasizes setting limits, avoiding impulsive spending, and understanding the potential impact of winning on your life. Remember, responsible play is paramount.

Part 2: Selecting Your Lucky Numbers:
- **Random vs. Pattern-Based:**

Discover the pros and cons of quick picks, random number generators, and the myth of "hot" and "cold" numbers. Explore pattern-based strategies like analyzing past winning numbers and using mathematical formulas, understanding their limitations.

- **Wheeling and Syndicates:**

Increase your odds by covering more numbers through wheeling techniques. Learn about forming syndicates, their legal and financial aspects, and the importance of clear communication and agreements.

Part 3: Advanced Strategies and Techniques:
- **Software & Analysis Tools:**

Evaluate the effectiveness of lottery software and data analysis tools, while emphasizing responsible use and understanding their limitations.

- **Syndicates and Game Theory:**

Explore finding reputable syndicates, legal and tax implications, and the importance of clear communication. Delve into game theory and psychology to make informed decisions while maintaining a balanced approach.

Part 4: Responsible Play and Financial Management:

- **Budgeting and Financial Planning:**

Learn to set realistic spending limits, prioritize financial obligations and goals, and avoid impulse purchases and debt. This section emphasizes responsible financial management, even before a potential win.

- **Winning Windfalls Wisely:**

Understand the importance of seeking professional financial advice, managing windfalls responsibly, avoiding scams, and investing for long-term security. Remember, a win shouldn't jeopardize your financial well-being.

- **Winning Reality and Responsible Enjoyment:**

Manage expectations by understanding the true odds and potential impact of winning on your life. Emphasize responsible wealth management and remember, the lottery is entertainment, not a guaranteed path to riches.

- **Finding Joy in the Game:**

Approach the lottery as a fun activity, not a get-rich-quick scheme. Focus on the enjoyment of the game and responsible participation. Remember, the journey itself can be rewarding.

"Six Numbers to Freedom" empowers you to approach the lottery with informed choices, responsible strategies, and a healthy perspective. Remember, responsible play is the true winning ticket!

Remember, the lottery is a form of entertainment, not a guaranteed path to wealth. Play responsibly and enjoy the ride!

www.ingramcontent.com/pod-product-compliance
Lightning Source LLC
Chambersburg PA
CBHW071050290526
45795CB00004B/1409